The Encyclopedia of Collectibles

TIME LIFE BOOKS®

Other Publications:
Library of Health
Classics of The Old West
The Epic of Flight
The Good Cook
The Seafarers
The Great Cities
World War II
Home Repair and Improvement
The World's Wild Places
The Time-Life Library of Boating
Human Behavior
The Art of Sewing
The Old West
The Emergence of Man
The American Wilderness
The Time-Life Encyclopedia of Gardening
Life Library of Photography
This Fabulous Century
Foods of the World
Time-Life Library of America
Time-Life Library of Art
Great Ages of Man
Life Science Library
The Life History of the United States
Time Reading Program
Life Nature Library
Life World Library
Family Library:
   How Things Work in Your Home
   The Time-Life Book of the Family Car
   The Time-Life Family Legal Guide
   The Time-Life Book of Family Finance

The Encyclopedia of Collectibles
Advertising Giveaways to Baskets

TIME-LIFE BOOKS, ALEXANDRIA, VIRGINIA

Time-Life Books Inc.
is a wholly owned subsidiary of
TIME INCORPORATED

Founder: Henry R. Luce 1898-1967

Editor-in-Chief: Henry Anatole Grunwald
President: J. Richard Munro
Chairman of the Board: Ralph P. Davidson
Executive Vice President: Clifford J. Grum
Chairman, Executive Committee: James R. Shepley
Editorial Director: Ralph Graves
Group Vice President, Books: Joan D. Manley
Vice Chairman: Arthur Temple

The Encyclopedia of Collectibles
was created under the supervision
of Time-Life Books by
TREE COMMUNICATIONS, INC.
President: Rodney Friedman
Publisher: Bruce Michel
Vice President: Ronald Gross
Secretary: Paul Levin

For information about any Time-Life book, please write:
Reader Information
Time-Life Books
541 North Fairbanks Court
Chicago, Illinois 60611

Library of Congress Cataloguing in Publication Data
Main entry under title:
  The encyclopedia of collectibles.
  Includes bibliographies.
  1. Americana. 2. Antiques — United States.
  I. Time-Life Books.
NK805.E63   745.1'09'0973   77-99201
ISBN 0-8094-2764-8
ISBN 0-8094-2763-X lib. bdg.
ISBN 0-8094-2762-1 retail ed.

©1978 Time-Life Books Inc. All rights reserved.
No part of this book may be reproduced in any form or by
any electronic or mechanical means, including information
storage and retrieval devices or systems, without prior
written permission from the publisher, except that brief
passages may be quoted for reviews.
Fifth printing. Revised 1981.
Published simultaneously in Canada.
School and library distribution by Silver Burdett Company,
Morristown, New Jersey.

TIME-LIFE is a trademark of Time Incorporated U.S.A.

Printed in U.S.A.

TIME-LIFE BOOKS INC.
Managing Editor: Jerry Korn
Executive Editor: David Maness
Assistant Managing Editors: Dale M. Brown
(planning), George Constable,
Thomas H. Flaherty Jr. (acting), Martin Mann,
John Paul Porter
Art Director: Tom Suzuki
Chief of Research: David L. Harrison
Director of Photography: Robert G. Mason
Assistant Art Director: Arnold C. Holeywell
Assistant Chief of Research: Carolyn L. Sackett
Assistant Director of Photography: Dolores A. Littles

Chairman: John D. McSweeney
President: Carl G. Jaeger
Executive Vice Presidents: John Steven Maxwell,
David J. Walsh
Vice Presidents: George Artandi (comptroller);
Stephen L. Bair (legal counsel); Peter G. Barnes;
Nicholas Benton (public relations);
John L. Canova; Beatrice T. Dobie (personnel);
Carol Flaumenhaft (consumer affairs);
James L. Mercer (Europe/South Pacific);
Herbert Sorkin (production); Paul R. Stewart
(marketing)

The Encyclopedia of Collectibles
Managing Editor: Andrea DiNoto
Text Director: Jay Gold
Art Director: Marsha Gold
Photographers: David Arky, Steven Mays
Assistant Editors: Cathy Cashion,
Linda Campbell Franklin, Richard Frostig,
Dennis Southers
Designers: Sonja Douglas, Christopher Jones
Administrative Assistant: Eva Gold
Writers: Peter Andrews, Sally Clark,
Douglas Ewing, William C. Ketchum Jr.,
Jerry E. Patterson, Mary Grace Skurka, Judy Wade

Consultants for this volume: Lester Barnett,
John Hoffman (Advertising Giveaways);
Robert Bishop (American Eagles); Mike Barrier
(Animation Film Art); Harmer Johnson
(Arrowheads); Albert Christian Revi (Art Glass
and Art Pottery); Gary Stradling (Art Pottery);
Don Berkebile (Automobilia); George Wintress
(Banks); Robert Walther (Barbed Wire); William
C. Ketchum Jr., George O. Bird (Baskets).

The Cover: The enormous range of art
glass *(page 54)* — in shape, size, color and
use — is indicated in this sampling.

The Encyclopedia of Collectibles
Editor: Betsy Frankel
Researchers: Bill Banks, Charlie Clark, Phyllis Wise
Editorial Assistant: Susan Sivard

Editorial Production
Production Editor: Douglas B. Graham
Operations Manager: Gennaro C. Esposito,
Gordon E. Buck (assistant)
Assistant Production Editor: Feliciano Madrid
Quality Control: Robert L. Young (director),
James J. Cox (assistant), Daniel J. McSweeney,
Michael G. Wight (associates)
Art Coordinator: Anne B. Landry
Copy Staff: Susan B. Galloway (chief), Ricki Tarlow,
Celia Beattie
Traffic: Kimberly K. Lewis

Correspondents: Elisabeth Kraemer (Bonn); Margot
Hapgood, Dorothy Bacon, Lesley Coleman
(London); Susan Jonas, Lucy T. Voulgaris (New
York); Maria Vincenza Aloisi, Josephine du
Brusle (Paris); Ann Natanson (Rome). Valuable
assistance was also provided by: Judy Aspinall,
Karin B. Pearce (London); Carolyn T. Chubet,
Miriam Hsia, Christina Lieberman (New York);
Mimi Murphy (Rome).

Acknowledgments: For help in the preparation of
this book, the editors wish to thank the following:
Alfred Burkiewicz, Michelle Cinotti, Betty DuPree,
Smith Hempstone Oliver, Ahuva Rabani, Edith
Rudman, Paul Sigman, Dave Smith. Advertising
giveaways pictured on pages 8 *(bottom left),* 10, 14,
15 *(left and top right),* from the collection of Roger
Steckler; photos from the *Index of American Design,*
pages 24-25, courtesy of The National Gallery of
Art, Washington, D.C.; coin, page 21, courtesy of
The Chase Manhattan Bank; cels of Betty Boop
and Porky Pig, page 40, courtesy of Helene
Pollack; pottery marks, page 84, and list of
American art potteries, page 85, reproduced by
permission of Charles Scribner's Sons, New York,
from *Art Pottery of the United States* by Paul Evans;
Benjamin Franklin autograph and forgery, page
97, courtesy of Charles Hamilton Galleries,
New York; Buzz Aldrin autograph, page 100,
reproduced by permission; painting by Walter M.
Baumhofer, page 135, used by permission of The
Cattleman, Fort Worth, Texas; Glidden
Advertisement, page 135, courtesy of the Baker
Library, Harvard University, Cambridge,
Massachusetts; Indian Baskets, page 157, courtesy
of Joel and Kate Kopp. Page 34, upper left, by
permission of The Bobbs-Merrill Company,
Incorporated; Copyright 1941, Paramount
Pictures, Incorporated.

Contents

  6 **Advertising Giveaways**
20 **American Eagles**
32 **Animation Film Art**
42 **Arrowheads**
54 **Art Glass**
70 **Art Pottery**
88 **Autographs**
102 **Automobilia**
116 **Banks**
128 **Barbed Wire**
138 **Baseball Cards**
150 **Baskets**

Advertising Giveaways
Gimcracks to Cherish

The free calendar from a local bank, the pen imprinted with an insurance agent's name and the hallmarked shopping bag from a fashionable store are perhaps the most familiar examples of that ubiquitous item of modern commerce, the useful trifle given away free to encourage a customer's trade. It is big business today: one company alone spends more than one million dollars annually for goodwill offerings that include, among other things, two million calendars and 7,000 dozen golf balls imprinted with its name. And giveaways were comparatively bigger business in times past, before there were television and radio commercials. Lavish illustrations and decorations, striking color lithography and often amusing advertising messages make these bits of trivia prime collectibles. Some are easy to find, for so many were made that they are likely to reward the search of almost any closet or drawer. Others are rare, and it is not unusual for a sought-after tray or pocket mirror to command a price as high as $1,000.

To collectors, a giveaway—handed out with no charge and generally no requirement for purchase—is distinguished from a premium, which is offered only in

The girl on this paper fan promoted Borden milk products in the 1890s.

Howard and Flo Fertig have amassed so many advertising giveaways in 20 years of collecting that the foyer and family room of their home, where the collection is displayed, looks like an old general store.

---

return for a nominal payment of cash or its equivalent in box tops or what not. (See *Premiums* in a separate volume.) And old giveaways are generally more desirable than those of recent vintage. This is partly because they are understandably rarer, but also because most are of higher quality—made of finer materials, such as metals, mother-of-pearl or Celluloid rather than modern plastic—and more colorfully designed and decorated. We look for things made anytime from the late 1890s through the Great Depression of the 1930s, but other collectors extend their interest to items from the 1940s.

We became collectors of advertising giveaways at about the same time we began to collect memorabilia connected with old-fashioned country stores and soda fountains. The two seemed to go together. Wherever we found biscuit bins and syrup dispensers we also ran across calendars for Hood's sarsaparilla and thermometers extolling Colburn's mustard or Occident flour. Over the years our collection of these giveaways eclipsed the store fittings, for the field is huge. But we have discovered from experience that some categories are more collectible than others.

The easiest giveaways to find are those that were handed out wholesale to all comers, such as calendars. In addition, calendars have been distributed by every kind of business, from giant insurance companies to neighborhood grocery stores. Our own favorites are the calendars given away by C. I. Hood Company of Lowell, Massachusetts, advertising its sarsaparilla *(opposite)*. Hood printed between six and seven million of these a year between 1891 and 1920, and we have a collection of 18 of them. The 1897 Hood's calendar came with coupons, one for each month, which could be redeemed for booklets, games, puzzles and other goodies. A second coupon calendar, issued a year later, was touted by Hood as a "$12 million gift to the American people" (that was the value placed on the premiums).

As much a necessity as the calendar, in the days before air conditioning, was the hand fan, and it too was produced and given away in abundance. Hand fans were made of paper, cardboard, straw and Celluloid,

A duplicate of this calendar for Hood's sarsaparilla (right) could be obtained in 1896 for six cents; three quarters of a century later, one sold for $20.

Hood's Sarsaparilla   Calendar 1896

Copyrighted 1895 by C.I. Hood & Co. Lowell, Mass. U.S.A.

HOOD'S
SARSAPARILLA
1896 CALENDAR

ONE COPY OF THIS CALENDAR SENT FOR 6c OR TWO FOR 10c. BY C.I. HOOD & CO. LOWELL MASS. U.S.A.

8 / ADVERTISING GIVEAWAYS

and like much advertising matter then and now were often decorated with pictures of appealing children and attractive women—no matter how tenuous their connection with the product. The fans were given away by the carload to church groups, funeral parlors and fraternal organizations and carried home from social and sporting events so often that it is a rare attic that does not contain one or two examples.

The advent of a new material—Celluloid, the ivory-like forerunner of modern plastics—stimulated the production in huge quantities of a variety of small items with diverse uses. One, the pin-back button, was useless except as advertising, and presumably appealed solely because it was a new kind of personal decoration. So many pin-back buttons were produced that some people collect nothing else. The button, made with an ingenious hoop spring that snapped into the back, was a popular advertising medium for everything from food to major appliances. There were buttons for Ceresota flour and Horlick's malted milk powder, for Dokash stoves, Starrett's tools and Bijur Brother pianos.

Collectors often assemble these buttons in sets. Some popular subjects are clothing (Red Goose shoes), farm machinery (John Deere), products named for the Yellow Kid comic strip (Yellow Kid ginger wafers, Yel-

A turn-of-the-century paperweight, 3½ inches in diameter, has a mirror on the reverse side. Characteristically, it uses the likeness of an attractive girl as a come-on for sausage.

Santa Claus buttons, given away at Christmas by department stores and banks, are a subspecialty among button collectors.

Handsomely printed Celluloid buttons, ¾ to 3½ inches across, made their wearers walking advertisements for everything from soap to dairy equipment. The buttons, called pin-backs, fastened to clothing by means of a wire pin that snapped under the rim.

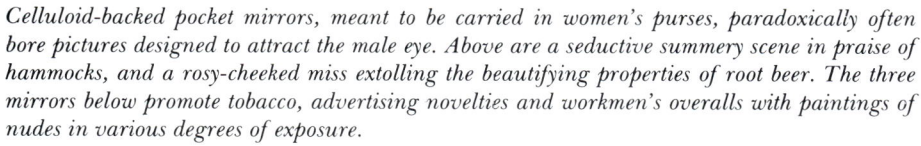

ADVERTISING GIVEAWAYS / 9

Celluloid-backed pocket mirrors, meant to be carried in women's purses, paradoxically often bore pictures designed to attract the male eye. Above are a seductive summery scene in praise of hammocks, and a rosy-cheeked miss extolling the beautifying properties of root beer. The three mirrors below promote tobacco, advertising novelties and workmen's overalls with paintings of nudes in various degrees of exposure.

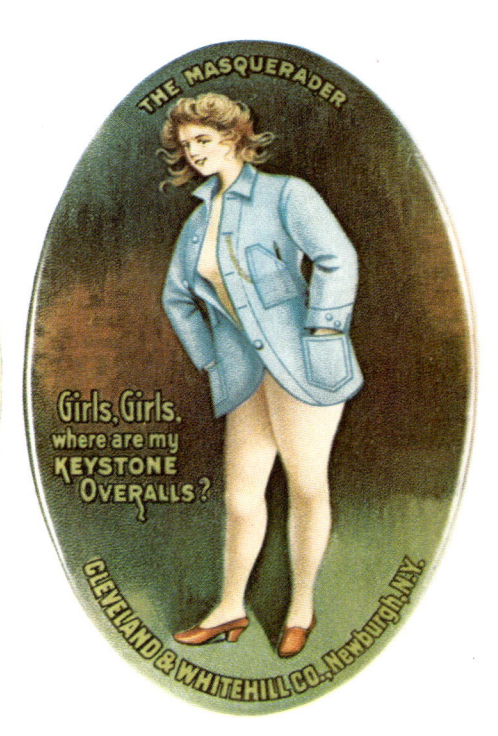

10 / ADVERTISING GIVEAWAYS

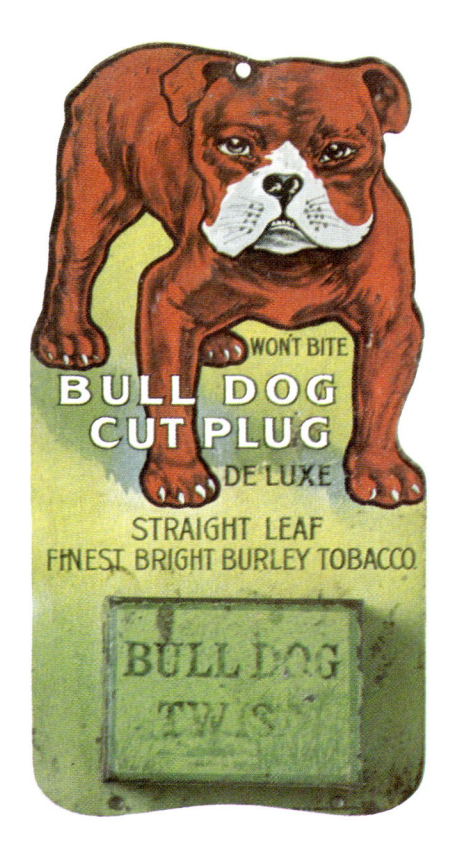

Matchsafes like these, which store wooden matches, frequently had pictures bearing a tenuous connection to the products they advertised—for the one at left, dog food.

Matches were kept in the base of this wall-mounted tin holder promoting tobacco.

Kid bubble gum), and the Santa Claus buttons *(page 8)* issued by department stores at Christmastime. A rare group of pin-back buttons are those connected with firearms (Peter's gunpowder and shells, Dupont gunpowder, Winchester rifles). Also valued for their rarity are the pin-back buttons, 7/8 to 1¼ inches across, issued during the mid-1920s. At that time manufacturers began to print their designs directly on the tin backing, and were using fewer colors and simpler designs.

The principal producers of pin-back buttons were the Whitehead & Hoag Company of Newark, New Jersey—which patented the first in 1896—American Artworks of Cochocton, Ohio, the St. Louis Button Company, and Bastian Brothers of Rochester, New York, which later bought out Whitehead & Hoag. Sometimes their names may still be found on the small circle of paper that was pressed into the back of the button—although by now most of these handy identifications have either been peeled off or have fallen off. When they are present they are a clue to age, for in addition to the manufacturer's name they include a patent date.

The same group of manufacturers, along with two others in Chicago, the Parisian Novelty Company and the Cruver Manufacturing Company, used their experience with Celluloid to popularize another giveaway: the Celluloid-backed pocket mirror. Round, oval or rectangular in shape and less than 3 inches across, the colorful mirrors ballyhooed everything from patent medicines to vaudeville shows. Unlike buttons, however, they are valued more for their condition than for their subject matter. Mirrors broke and their Celluloid backing got scratched and dented; their designs wore off and moisture seeped under the rim, staining or "foxing" the Celluloid. So rare is it to find mirrors in good condition that the collection of Al and Jean Zerries, source of the illustrations on page 9, is considered a great prize. All of the Zerries' 250 mirrors, collected over eight years, are in near-perfect condition.

The rarity of good mirrors has created a brisk business in reproductions, and collectors should be wary. One way to spot a copy is to examine the edge: the plastic used for reproductions frequently puckers or crimps as it tucks under the rim. Celluloid seldom did. An authentic pocket mirror also carries, nine times out of 10, the name of its maker imprinted on the rim just at the mirror edge; in fact, it is sometimes half hidden under the mirror. Sometimes the manufacturer also included, along with his name, an offer to supply a duplicate mirror for two to six cents in stamps—a fairly reliable sign that it is an early mirror.

Celluloid also went into measuring-tape cases, pin holders and matchsafes. Flammable Celluloid was not perhaps the best of all materials to use for a match holder, which may be why a second version appeared: a

ADVERTISING GIVEAWAYS / 11

Small tip trays, used to present the customer with his change in bars and restaurants, vary in shape from oval, above, in praise of Clysmic table water, to the intricately die-cut indented Indian head, 5 inches across, that advertised Modox, an herb beverage. More common was the circular tray, like the two below. The 1904 Coca-Cola tray, 6 inches across, portrays actress Hilda Clark, who also posed for other Coca-Cola advertising. Moxie, a rival of Coca-Cola, at one time outsold it with a variety of persuasive claims like the one on this tray.

12 / ADVERTISING GIVEAWAYS

A patriotic young miss on a 12-inch serving tray lauds a brand of phosphate, an effervescent beverage containing a little phosphorus.

ADVERTISING GIVEAWAYS / 13

A far-fetched "Indian maiden" waves the flag for Northwestern Brewery on a tray made by the Tuscarora Advertising Company.

14 / ADVERTISING GIVEAWAYS

Small Celluloid advertising novelties come in so many forms that a collection could be built of them alone. These six, all relatively rare, are, from the left: a scorekeeper for baseball fans; a tatting shuttle for making lace; a paperweight turtle with a metal body; a stamp case that contains moisture-absorbent material to keep stamps from sticking together; folding toothpicks; and a shoehorn.

small metal box with a Celluloid wrapper. The bottom of these metal matchsafes contained a striking surface. A third form of match holder much favored by advertisers was made of tin and contained a raised compartment for wooden matches, along with a rough surface to strike them on *(page 10)*. It was meant to be hung on the kitchen wall next to the stove—a daily reminder of the advertiser's identity.

In contrast to such trinkets as matchsafes and pinback buttons are the very practical, very handsome and much sought-after metal trays. The biggest users of trays for advertising purposes have always been the beverage industries, and the trays have been of two types. Some were serving trays; but there was also a smaller size, 4½ to 6 inches across, used by waiters and waitresses to present change and to receive tips. In some restaurants and taverns the tip tray was placed beside the cash register for the same purpose.

The serving trays—round, oval or rectangular—ran in size from 9¾ to 25 inches across. When not in use, they stood upright against the back of the bar or soda fountain, where they formed an attractive display. Mindful of this, advertisers featured pictures of fashionable women and stage personalities, and generally kept their commercial messages simple, limiting them to the name of the product and a slogan rimming the edge of the tray. Before government agencies clamped down on medical claims in advertising, Coca-Cola's trays bore the legend, "A Specific for Headache," while Moxie's advertised, "Feeds the Nerves." Coca-Cola trays, which now command the highest prices, often bore designs from well-known illustrators like Norman Rockwell.

Trays signed by artists with familiar names are naturally considered valuable. But so are trays that are otherwise hard to find. Brewery trays, for example, were probably made in the greatest number and variety. Yet brewery trays can be expensive because of the hiatus in their production during Prohibition, between 1919 and 1933. Other trays commanding high prices are the relative few that advertise products other than beverages—tobacco, ice cream, patent medicine or coffee.

The value of a tray is also determined by age, and not simply because older trays are rarer. The early ones were produced by old-fashioned lithography, a time-consuming and expensive process that results in colors richer and more brilliant than those applied by the faster and cheaper photolithographic process that became common at about the time of World War I.

The name of the lithographer, which usually appears near the rim, offers one clue to the age of the tray (they are still being manufactured and the new ones, naturally, are not worth much). Most of the major manufacturers operated within a specific period. The Tuscarora Company and the Standard Advertising Company, for

ADVERTISING GIVEAWAYS / 15

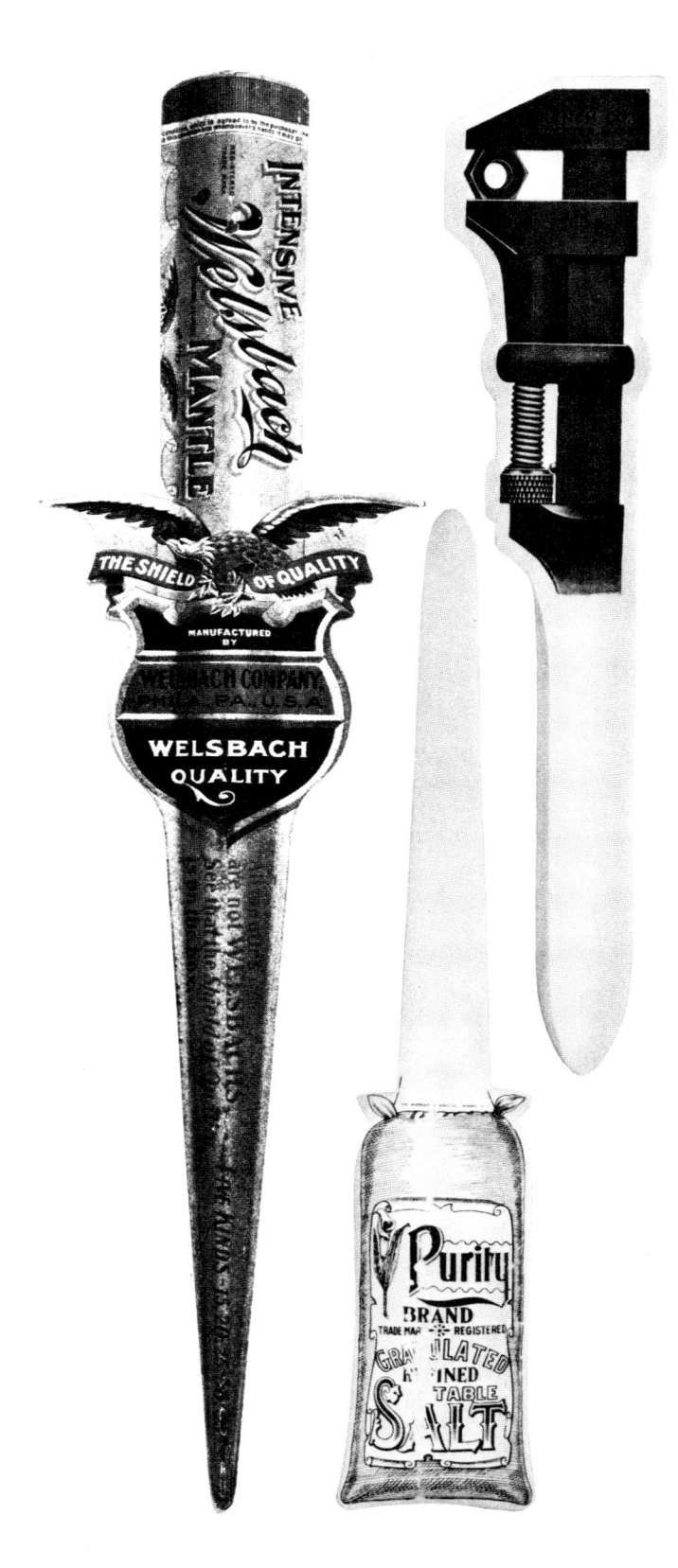

Die-cut Celluloid bookmarks had space for advertising, including poetry in praise of Welsbach gas mantles. Carnation milk and Standard plumbing fixtures gave bookmarks as souvenirs of expositions.

The silhouette of a metal gas mantle, a bag of salt and a monkey wrench, both Celluloid, supplied the outlines for three letter openers, given away by their respective manufacturers.

A sampling of easy-to-find giveaways that can be collected inexpensively includes, clockwise from top left, a buttonhook, a milk-bottle opener, a stickpin, a button-sized money clip and a lapel pin.

16 / ADVERTISING GIVEAWAYS

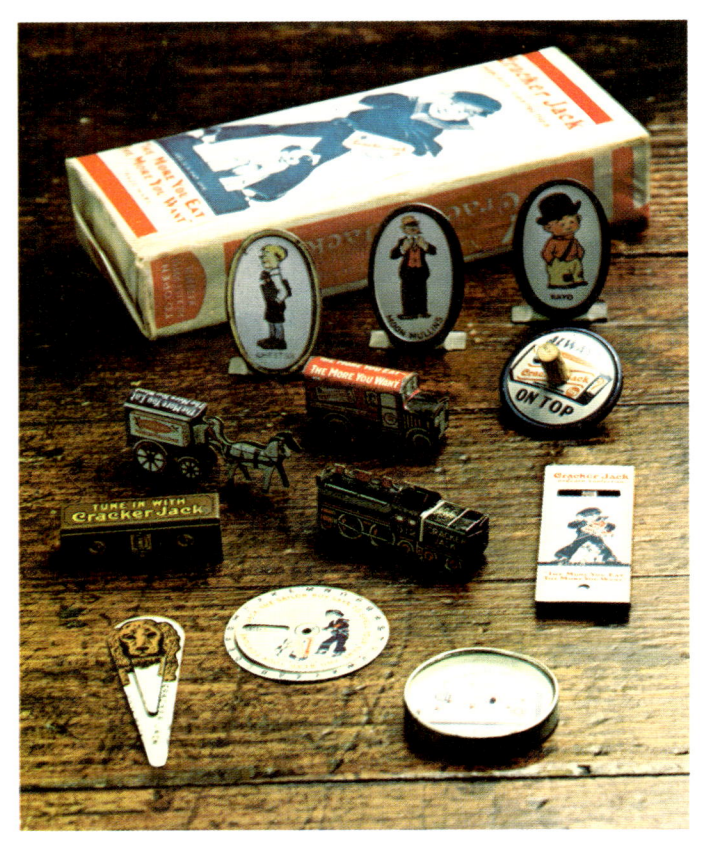

Cracker Jack prizes have included, clockwise from the top, tin comic-strip characters, a spinning top, a tin whistle in the shape of the Cracker Jack box, a ball-in-hole game, a fortunetelling game, a bookmark, a miniature radio console and three miniature tin vehicles.

In this array of tin toys given away as advertisements in the 1920s are, from the top, a pipe whistle, a row of three wooden-handled tops, and a row including a whistle, a roulette wheel and two cricket noisemakers. The bottom row contains two yellow whistles.

instance, both started manufacturing trays in Coshocton, Ohio, in the 1880s. Subsequent mergers and separations resulted in the Meek & Beech Company and then in the H. D. Beech Company and the Meek Company, all dating from the turn of the century. In 1909 the Meek Company became American Artworks, and after 1930 trays by the latter were stamped with the name of a subsidiary, American Colortype Company.

Tin trays were one of the chief "sales stimulators" given away to storekeepers to induce them to handle a manufacturer's products. In addition to trays, there were holders for wrapping twine, measuring bowls for dipping crackers from a barrel *(page 17)* and more elaborate gifts: coffee grinders bearing the coffee's name; thermometers and barometers in praise of soft drinks, tobacco, medicines and starch; even wall clocks. Some of these old clocks are still around—those for Sauer's extracts and Croft's Swiss Milk Cocoa, for instance—but they disappear into collections with lightning speed and are not easy to find.

Special customers were often moved with special giveaways. The toys packaged for children in boxes of Cracker Jack, the caramel-coated popcorn confection, are probably the most famous of these. In the old days these toys were generally produced in sets—of trucks, for instance, or of puzzles, games, tops or comic-strip characters *(above, left)*. We have collected about 40 Cracker Jack toys, but have not yet found all 10 free-standing pictures of comic-strip characters produced in the 1920s. We have Harold Teen, Smitty, Kayo, Skeezix, Chester and Moon Mullins, but we lack Little Orphan Annie, Uncle Walt, Herbie and Perry Winkle.

Cracker Jack toys first appeared in 1912, but the notion of offering giveaways designed especially for children began a few years earlier. Savings banks—either food containers designed for later use as banks or miniature replicas of actual food products—were offered as early as 1910 and continued to be offered into the 1930s and '40s. Some of the banks were flimsy constructions of cardboard, with metal used only for the tops, bottoms and seams, but enough of them have survived to make them good collectibles.

Children's booklets, many of them very nicely printed, have also had a long history as giveaways. Some were

ADVERTISING GIVEAWAYS / 17

Tin-can banks, 2 to 3 inches tall, promoted both thrift and the manufacturer's product. Two of the cans, for Ocean Spray sauce and Bab-O cleanser, are replicas of the actual package.

Given to grocers, this 4-inch-deep china bowl scooped biscuits from a barrel.

A blotter cover advertising peanuts was intended to convince retailers of the selling power of the name of a famous child film star of the 1920s.

A pin holder given away by a cafeteria holds dressmakers' pins, gives birthstone information and has a pocket mirror on the back.

Giveaways designed for soda-fountain proprietors included a stoneware mug for Lash's root beer, an English china mug decorated with the Hires root-beer boy, and two flower-trimmed china cups for serving Rexsoma and Vigoral, two hot beef-extract drinks.

18 / ADVERTISING GIVEAWAYS

A coloring book for children, issued by Ceresota flour in 1912, relates the adventures of Ceresota, son of Ceres, the goddess of grain. The boy on the book cover is the same boy shown slicing a huge loaf of bread on the flour sack, Ceresota's trademark since 1912.

coloring books; others were books of rhymes, stories and fairy tales. In 1915 Wrigley's gum put out a popular rhyming-coloring book based on Mother Goose:

> One, two, it's good to chew
> Three, four, they all want more
> Five, six, it comes in sticks
> Seven, eight, the flavor's great
> Nine, ten, guess again . . . it's Wrigley's.

Since most of these gimcracks were given away in astronomical numbers, you are almost sure to find a few by looking through closets and attics in the homes of friends and relatives, but not enough to build a serious collection. We have found some of our giveaways by prowling through old buildings that look as though they might once have served as warehouses. Old, abandoned country stores are another rich source, but they are hard to find now. Once we discovered a country store in Pennsylvania that was closed but not dismantled. We could see through the windows that it was a collector's dream, but it took us 10 years to get inside. It belonged to people whose family had owned it continuously for 106 years. The store yielded a gold mine of giveaways—among them, all 18 of our Hood calendars.

We also find our giveaways through the more obvious channels: antique dealers, auctions, flea markets, ads in collectors' journals. Flea markets are an especially fruitful source. When we go to the outdoor Brimfield, Massachusetts, flea market, which draws 700 dealers and is the largest in the country, we get up before dawn to arrive in good time, and we spend nine or 10 hours browsing. There are also three semiannual shows devoted to advertising giveaways where more than 100 dealers come together under one roof. They are held in Gaithersburg, Maryland, in September and February; in Indianapolis, usually in September and March; and in Los Angeles, usually in October and June.

One thing to be wary of when buying from dealers—whether at shows, flea markets or shops—is lack of

A 1915 Mother Goose issued by Wrigley's gum urged: "Jack be nimble, Jack be quick; Jack, run and get your Wrigley stick."

authenticity. It is easy to copy giveaways, which were cheaply made to start with, and copiers can be ingenious. They often stain or dent wares intentionally, for instance, and have even gone so far as to soak tin in horse urine to create a pitted effect. For this reason, it is a good idea to avoid any blistered or stained tinware unless the dealer is willing to supply a written statement of its authenticity.

A magnifying glass is a useful tool for checking authenticity. The design on a tray reproduced by modern methods of photolithography, for instance, will show up as a pattern of dots of uniform size, like the dots on a newspaper photograph. In older forms of photolithography, the pattern of dots is stippled and irregular.

Company histories may also be helpful in tracking down proof of age. Often these histories include information on how products were advertised and marketed during a particular period. A few manufacturers even keep files of their catalogues and sample cards: Coca-Cola, for instance, has extensively documented its advertising programs, and many breweries also maintain useful archives.

Because advertising giveaways were ephemeral even when they were made, they were seldom treated with care and frequently need some restoration. We clean our metal and Celluloid giveaways with a soft cloth and a special liquid wax called Sani-Wax, but you can use a silicone car wax—one that contains no abrasives. Waxing not only cleans the article, but often restores some of the original brightness of its colors. Before waxing, we also remove small rust spots on tin by sanding them, a section at a time, with No. 40 steel wool.

Then, to preserve our collection we keep it out of the sunlight, which can cause Celluloid to crack and peel, and mirrors to break. In winter we use a humidifier to minimize dryness and we keep mirrors and small objects in glass cases to protect them from dampness—and to cut down on the dusting chore. We also avoid stacking objects if possible because so many giveaways have finishes that are easily chipped or scratched.

Although caring for our collection is in a sense a labor of love, we also do it for practical reasons. Because of the growing number of collectors in this field, the law of supply and demand has sent prices soaring. A soda-fountain dispenser for Fowler's Cherry Smash that we bought in 1974 for $35 was worth $500 just three years later. We are naturally happy about that, but we are also happy to think that as giveaways continue to increase in value, more and more of them will be saved from destruction—to testify to the resourcefulness and ingenuity of American businessmen.

MUSEUMS
Warshaw Collection of Business Americana
Museum of History and Technology
Smithsonian Institution
Washington, D.C. 20560

COLLECTORS ORGANIZATIONS
National Association of Breweriana Advertising
c/o John Murray
475 Old Surrey Road
Hinsdale, Illinois 60521

BOOKS
Hake, Ted, *The Button Book*. Dafran House, 1973

Hammond, Dorothy, with Robert Hammond, *Collectible Advertising*. Wallace-Homestead, 1974

Munsey, Cecil, *The Illustrated Guide to Collectibles of Coca-Cola*. Hawthorn Books Inc., 1972

Muzio, Jack, *Collectible Tin Advertising Trays*. Brandes Press, 1971

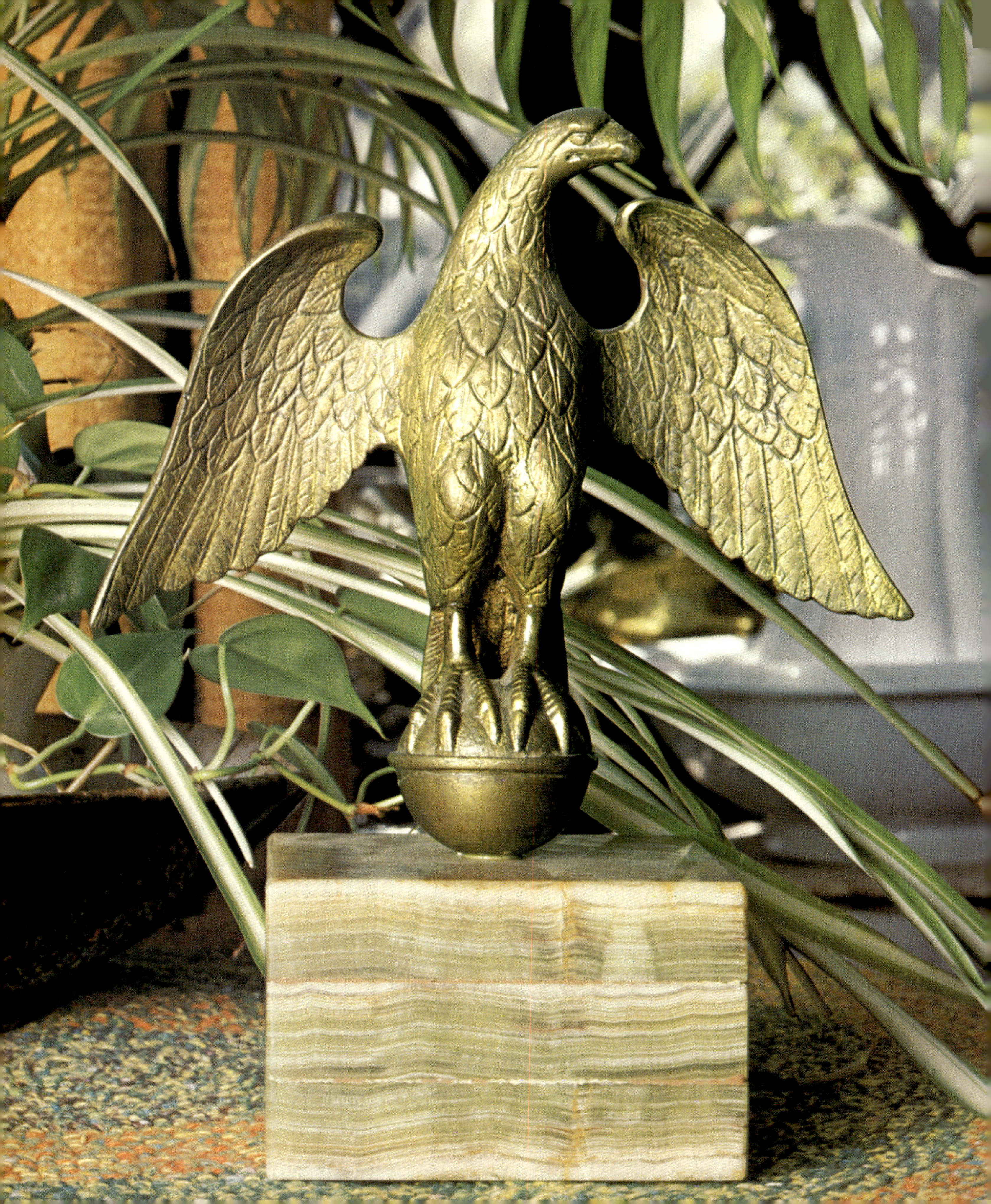

American Eagles
Ubiquitous Emblem of the Republic

I became a collector of eagles during World War I, when eagle motifs were everywhere—as they always seem to be in times of national crisis and national celebration. There were eagles on recruiting posters, on magazine covers and in cartoons. Most directly, there were eagles on my person. They decorated the cap insignia and brass buttons of my uniform as a second lieutenant in the U.S. Army.

Like most collectors, I was drawn to my subject partly by its historical associations: the eagle has played a long

Clarence P. Hornung has written 25 books on design, antiques and history, including "The American Eagle in Art and Design." He is often greeted at museums with, "There's that eagle man again."

and fascinating role as a potent patriotic emblem. As an artist, however, I was also attracted to the eagle by the beauty of its shape, and by its expressiveness. The curved beak, sinuous neck, powerful torso and exquisitely feathered wings offer an extraordinary range of possibilities for representation. Transformed into a symbol, the eagle can be proud, dignified, ferocious, aggressive, unassailable. Shown in repose, it can be the embodiment of stillness; shown in flight, it is the quintessence of motion.

At first, my eagle collection was practical. I was planning to make a career in advertising design, and like all commercial artists I needed to build up a "swipe file"—a collection of photographs and clippings from magazines to serve as inspiration for drawing all kinds of subjects. So the nucleus of my eagle collection was illustrative material. More than half a century later, those first few pictures have grown into a collection of thousands of items, including a great many that are not illustrations. I collect anything and everything having to do with American eagles in every conceivable medium—sculpture, painting, wood carving, glass, iron, brass and cloth. And I have concluded that this single subject may well be inexhaustible. The eagle may be seen decorating

Mounted on a marble base, this 7-inch cast-brass eagle was made in the second half of the 19th Century as the ornamental top of a flagpole. It is the type seen when the flag is carried in a parade.

wallpaper, ladies' bandboxes, musical instruments, drapery fabrics, jugs and glassware, drawer pulls, playing cards, butter molds, tavern signs and iron stoves—to name only a very few. In official use, it appears on ship figureheads, on coins, atop flagstaffs, and as monumental sculptures on the façades of official buildings. You will also find one on the back of every dollar bill in your pocketbook or wallet.

How does one go about starting a collection devoted to an object that appears in so many guises, and to which no general rules of excellence or value apply? My advice would be to begin by looking at eagles in photographs, to gain some feeling for the artistic inspiration that underlies the bird's use as a decorative device on various kinds of artifacts. Then I would take a trip to a nearby museum for an introduction to the scope and style of

The 1804 silver dollar, one of the rarest United States coins, bears a heraldic eagle on its reverse side. Only 15 of these coins are known to exist; one was sold for $225,000 in 1974.

22 / AMERICAN EAGLES

A silver brooch, 2 inches from the tip of the wing to the tail, shows an eagle bearing an olive branch. It dates from the turn of the century when patriotism was rampant.

the eagle's use throughout history. There is, so far as I know, no museum devoted solely to the eagle; but there are any number of museum collections in which the eagle appears. Eagle figureheads, for example, are on display at maritime museums, and eagle weather vanes can be viewed in collections such as those at the museum villages in Shelburne, Vermont, and Sturbridge, Massachusetts, or in various regional museums that feature antique farm equipment. The Abby Aldrich Rockefeller Folk Art Center, which is located in Williamsburg, Virginia, contains a particularly impressive collection of eagles in folk art, perhaps the single most costly and exciting area of eagle collecting.

One of the safer areas of eagle collecting for people who are concerned about verifying the value of items that are in their collection is coinage. This is because coin collectors and reputable coin dealers buy and sell within a relatively well-established framework of prices and guidelines to authenticity.

The eagle has a long history on American coinage. It first appeared, as a rather long-necked bird with outstretched wings, on a copper coin that was issued in New Jersey in 1786. The following year New York issued a penny that sported an eagle design resembling the one used on the Great Seal of the United States, which had been adopted in 1782, except that the profile on the coin faces right rather than left. The country's first gold coins were minted in 1795. Called eagles and half eagles, these were ten- and five-dollar pieces. On each, the eagle's wings are extended, and the bird carries a laurel wreath in its beak and a palm branch in its claws. A similar design was stamped on quarter eagles, which were valued then at $2.50 and released the following year, and on double eagles, which were minted in 1849—the famous twenty-dollar gold piece. Silver dollars, half dollars and half dimes entered circulation in 1794, showing a spread-winged eagle perched on a rock, and encircled by a laurel wreath.

Among the more unusual and valuable numismatic eagles are the silver dollars dated 1804 *(page 21)*. Like many 19th Century American coins, they reflect the diversity of styles permitted coin designers, who were at liberty to portray the eagle soaring or perched, wings folded, on a branch or rock. On this particular coin, the eagle strikes a heraldic pose, bearing in its beak a ribbon that reads *E Pluribus Unum*. Only 15 of these silver dollars were minted—and of that number only two were officially ordered by the U.S. government, for presentation as diplomatic gifts to heads of state in Asia and Arabia. The remaining coins somehow managed to be struck as "extras." To further complicate the mystery, most experts believe that the original coin was actually made in 1835 and then for some reason predated to read 1804. Except for the two that were ordered as gifts, the coins were never circulated, and they now bring astronomical prices.

Apart from their monetary value, eagle-bearing coins are intriguing because they frequently had an important, though difficult to trace, influence on the eagle designs that decorated all kinds of consumer goods. Few of the designers who lived and worked in cities had the opportunity to stalk the bird and observe it in the wild. And although John J. Audubon spent a number of years painting the eagle in its natural habitat, few craftsmen of the 19th Century could afford to purchase Audubon's splendidly detailed prints to use as source material for their designs. Consequently they turned to numismatic eagles for their models.

One class of consumer goods for which eagle motifs were especially popular was china and glass dinnerware. After the American Revolution, almost as soon as American sovereignty was clearly established, British potteries opportunely—and profitably—switched their export designs for the American market from flowers to eagles. The country's expanding trade with China, too, brought in quantities of hand-painted porcelain deco-

An eagle poster designed for the Citizens' Food Committee in 1947 urged Americans to be frugal in a time of postwar shortages.

AMERICAN EAGLES / 23

A Treasury of Authentic Eagles

Most people remember the WPA—the Works Progress Administration, established in the 1930s to relieve unemployment—for its ditch-digging and leaf-sweeping gangs, but the WPA also created jobs for actors, writers and artists. One of these projects assigned artists to create the "Index of American Design," a collection of reproductions recording the country's folk art. Naturally, eagles bulked large in the index—it included more than 100 examples, many of them wood carvings such as those shown here. Now in the National Gallery of Art in Washington, D.C., the index has become the most important source for authentic designs of the national emblem. Many of these have been included in the book compiled from the index, *Treasury of American Design*.

The carver exaggerated the head and claws of this fierce polychrome oak eagle, which originally decorated the pilothouse of a riverboat called the War Eagle, built in 1845 and berthed in Cincinnati.

John Haley Bellamy of Kittery, Maine, was a prolific creator of carved eagles. This one, with a monumental wingspread of nearly 19 feet, is believed to be the largest he ever made. It was done for the prow of the U.S.S. Lancaster, which it adorned from 1881 to 1913. After the Lancaster was decommissioned, the eagle was preserved in the Mariners Museum in Newport News, Virginia.

AMERICAN EAGLES / 25

A stern board made for a private yacht, the Dauntless, in 1874 displays an eagle with a 6-foot wingspread. The eagle, carved from pine, was originally covered with gold leaf but was repainted with gilt in 1937. The Dauntless now rests in Mystic, Connecticut.

This eagle, wings arched in flight, once perched atop the pilothouse on a tugboat. It is gilded and measures about 3 feet from the tip of its wings to the bottom of the globe base.

Painted eagles bearing the shield of the republic appeared on many Union Army drums during the Civil War. The snare drum above sounded marches and tattoos for the 9th Infantry Regiment.

rated with the national bird. At first, the eagle that was displayed on Chinese porcelain was a somewhat scrawny creature, but canny Chinese merchants soon learned to adapt their wares to American tastes, and produced nobler, healthier-looking birds.

With the improvements in the process of making pressed glass in the 1820s, another likely candidate for eagle designs emerged. A type of pressed glassware called American Lacy was introduced, with raised decorations like those seen on the finest cut glass. The American eagle was quickly adopted as a favorite decorative device for this ware, and appears often as a central design element, surrounded by elaborate traceries. My own collection includes a pressed-glass eagle cup-plate manufactured in 1831 by the Boston & Sandwich Glass Company.

American Lacy glass was a huge success and enormous quantities of it were made. Undoubtedly, much of it also got broken. A century later, the value of an original cup-plate like mine was about $25. But cheap replicas could be bought at the dime store for 25 cents, and the quality of the imitation was excellent *(opposite, top)*. The only way to tell the two versions apart is to examine the edge: in the older version the serrations are sharper. Also on the originals there are usually minuscule nicks, the inevitable result of age.

From about 1840 through the Civil War, the eagle appeared as a frequent decorative device on another sort of glass. More than 100 different whiskey bottles, chiefly pint-size flasks *(page 28)*, featured eagles. Normally they were further ornamented with patriotic slogans, scrolls, floral medallions, stars, sunbursts, the flag and other designs that struck the artists' fancies. Some flasks bore eagles on both sides, but many combined a likeness of the bird with a portrait of a popular President, such as Washington or Jackson. One of these 19th Century eagle bottles portrayed John Quincy Adams—a President so rarely honored in this way that any collector would be in luck to acquire it.

Apart from these commercially produced examples of eagle designs, there are also more space-consuming and expensive objects that provided opportunities for eagle ornamentation. Some of them are the creations of 18th and 19th Century master cabinetmakers. Collectors who combine a love of antique furniture with an interest in eagles, for instance, find that some of the most famous names in the field of woodworking and furniture designing are associated with the eagle motif. George Hepplewhite, Duncan Phyfe and Benjamin Randolph, among others, painted eagle designs on chair backs, carved them onto mirror frames, stamped them onto brass fittings and inlaid them into fine wood.

But the most intriguing examples of eagles created by craftsmen are, to my mind, those found in the realm of the folk artist. These native craftsmen and craftswomen, working at home or traveling about the country, were often extremely gifted, and created some of the finest renderings of eagles and other indigenous subjects I have ever seen. Some of these early American artists are anonymous; others achieved fame long after death. Most important for the contemporary collector, much of their work undoubtedly still remains to be discovered by lucky and observant enthusiasts who spend some time poking through the small antique shops and flea markets of rural America.

One wood carver who is often lumped together with folk artists—because his pieces are often included in collections of folk art—was actually a highly sophisticated, full-time sculptor named John Bellamy. By rights, Bellamy should be classified as a "fine artist." During his lifetime he carved hundreds of eagles, both large and small. His biggest piece is the 3,200-pound figurehead commissioned for the U.S.S. *Lancaster (page 24)*. But the best-known Bellamy eagles are carvings, usually about 2 feet across, worked in a combination of high and low relief. He used one plank to carve the wings, body and any decorative device, such as a shield, slogan-bearing ribbon or banner. The head and neck were then carved from a smaller block of wood, which, when attached to the background carving, projected from it to create dramatic shapes and shadows.

Eagles that were created by Bellamy seem to be flying straight at you—or, if you stand close to them, seem about to veer right past your ear. Bellamy eagles have been copied extensively and mass produced, which means that the prudent collector must be prepared to seek expert advice—or to acquire a thorough knowledge of how to date wood and paint, and of the fine points of Bellamy's style—to guarantee authenticity.

Two other men who command attention from eagle collectors are true folk artists: Wilhelm Schimmel and Aaron Mountz. Both men were solitary, itinerant wood carvers who wandered around the Pennsylvania countryside in the late 19th Century, often trading their work for nothing more than bed and board. And both created marvelously original specimens of American primitivism that are now highly prized by museums and collectors. Some Schimmels are signed, others are not; but anyone who chances across one of his bold eagles, with its irregular geometry and deep incisions, should not hesitate to buy it. He will acquire in a single stroke a superb piece of Americana and, at the same time, an object almost certain to increase in monetary value. Mountz's eagles were influenced by Schimmel's, but they tended to be more intricately worked and, in the eyes of some collectors, to lack the power and spontaneity of Schimmel's.

The largest wooden eagles, such as John Bellamy's

Two apparently identical pressed-glass eagle plates were actually made a century apart. The original, at left, was made by the Boston & Sandwich Glass Company of Massachusetts. The only difference in the 1920s reproduction is that its outlines are less definite.

These 3-inch brass eagle medallions were ornaments for furniture in the 1850s.

This cast-iron eagle was once a "snowbird," bolted on pitched roofs to stop snow slides. Mounted on a book end, it now supports books with eagle-decorated bindings.

28 / AMERICAN EAGLES

Pennsylvania German folk artists of the mid-19th Century carved these eagle butter molds of maple, a hardwood excellent for intricate details. The designs, in reverse relief, are 4½ inches across and were meant to be stamped on blocks of butter.

A pint-size whiskey flask shows an eagle with a Liberty legend, produced by the Willington Glass Company between 1847 and 1872.

This 32-inch stamped sheet-brass eagle was designed to be used as a decoration for speakers' platforms and parade floats in the mid-19th Century; a slot behind the eagle's body held five small flags. It was spotted by the author in a department-store window display during the 1939 New York World's Fair and, after repeated requests, was sold to him when the display was dismantled.

enormous birds created as figureheads for ships, were carved fully in the round. But there are also many smaller eagles carved in relief. Many vessels carried eagle carvings in the form of billethead or fiddlehead figures beneath the bowsprit, or as stern-board decorations *(page 25)*. And some of the more collectible carved eagles are those found on the small wooden objects that were produced by Pennsylvania carvers for household use. For example, butter molds *(far left)* whittled from maple, pine or poplar often display highly stylized designs. These were imprinted upon the surface of fresh butter brought to a farm table.

Closely related to these wooden butter molds in style are small eagle castings of iron and brass made at about the same time, and intended for use as trivets, ornaments for iron stoves, doorstops, drawer pulls and other types of decorative hardware. The similarity in style between the wooden and metal eagles resulted from the ironmaster's practice of fashioning his original pattern in wood, then transferring it to the sand mold that was to receive the molten metal. Bins or tubs of assorted junk metal in out-of-the-way antique stores are likely places to look for cast-iron eagles.

Another fascinating category of metal eagles is the weather vane fabricated from sheet copper, brass or tin. To catch the wind, such birds invariably have an exaggerated wingspan that ranges from 1 to 6 feet or more across. The larger sizes are now quite hard to find. The rarest of all eagle weather vanes, however, are the ones without any bullet holes: through the years few farm boys—or their fathers, for that matter—have been able to resist using these spinning eagles for occasional rounds of target practice.

Inside the farmhouse, wives and daughters made a more constructive contribution to eagle art work than their menfolk. Using needle and thread, they stitched the eagle into the designs of quilts and draperies and hooked it into rugs. Sometimes the eagle was the centerpiece of these textile creations; sometimes it was worked into the border. Usually the aquiline image was accompanied by stars, flowers, festoons, trees, houses or other decorative devices, and many of them are true triumphs of design. Fortunately for today's collectors, these domesticated examples of eagle folk art became treasured family heirlooms, passed down from generation to generation. Many of these works still exist, but they are apt to be expensive. And their value may be further enhanced by the seamstress' custom of stitching her name and the date of completion on the work.

The most fragile eagle collectibles are those printed on paper. Few newsprint eagles have survived from the 19th Century, although the printers' plates *(page 31)* from which they were made (first cut in wood, then cast in metal) are far more durable and do turn up from time to time. Old postcards and—even more surprisingly—antique cutout valentines also yield fascinating glimpses of the country's long interest in the national emblem. And in the back pages of penmanship manuals executed for school children by experts in Spencerian script you may come across pages devoted to elaborate scrolls and flourishes—often culminating in a beautifully rendered American eagle.

From this treasure trove of sources I have built an eagle collection that goes far beyond my original intention. My eagles, it is true, reflect my interest in art. But they have also led me into an exploration of the eagle as a symbol used not only by the American nation, but by people everywhere and in all times.

The ancient Persians, Egyptians, Medes and Assyrians all made use of the eagle as a symbol, identifying it with religious power and martial strength. Marching in conquest over the ancient world, the Roman legions were accompanied by standard-bearers carrying an eagle aloft, its wings uplifted, holding a thunderbolt of Jupiter. And in early Christian art the figure of the eagle was associated with the Mass, appearing, wings outspread, on a basket of bread signifying the Eucharist. Centuries later, Napoleon revived the thunderbolt-clutching eagle as the symbol of his short-lived empire, and his son, who never gained the throne, was known in childhood as l'Aiglon: the Eaglet.

The eagle found its symbolic way into American life only a couple of generations after the arrival of the *Mayflower*. Sometime between 1664 and 1710—the year New Yorke dropped the e from its name—an undated brass token carrying a representation of an eagle was issued as New York coinage. The year the Declaration of Independence was signed, New York state incorporated the bird on its state seal. It was General George Washington, however, who probably did the most to identify the eagle with the creation of the nation when he chose it as the motif for the buttons on his uniform during the Revolutionary War—thus initiating a tradition I fell heir to several wars later.

At his inauguration in 1789, Washington stood beneath a huge eagle that adorned the pediment of Federal Hall in New York City. And when the first President made a subsequent triumphal tour of the 13 states, he was greeted everywhere he went by all manner of eagle images. Eagles were traced on whitewashed windowpanes, behind which candles flickered to project an eerie aquiline silhouette into the night. At gala balls in the President's honor, ladies were seen carrying eagle-trimmed fans, and their escorts sported lapel pins that bore the image of an eagle. Posters and banners, too, displayed the visiting President's personal badge of military and political victories.

Washington's regard for the eagle's potent symbolism

30 / AMERICAN EAGLES

An assemblage of stamped-brass eagles, chiefly military ornaments, is displayed in a gilded frame. The two top eagles are 19th Century insignia meant for the shakos—or dress helmets—of artillery and infantry regiments. At left is a World War I officer's cap ornament; at right, a drawer pull. The large central shield, a regimental insignia, is flanked on the right by a Civil War insignia and on the left by a Napoleonic eagle on a belt buckle. The buttons at bottom are from U.S. Army uniforms of the 19th Century.

may have impressed other Founding Fathers. In 1782, after three unsuccessful attempts, the Continental Congress finally agreed on a design for the Great Seal of the United States, incorporating the eagle as its principal component. Thus official sanction was bestowed on the bird, despite demurrers from Benjamin Franklin, who favored the wild turkey, and Thomas Jefferson, who wanted to forgo feathered creatures altogether in favor of a Seal showing the Israelites fleeing from the bondage of the Pharaoh.

The American eagle shown on the Great Seal is more properly called the "bald eagle," though this term, too, is inaccurate. The bird shown, the only eagle indigenous to this country, has a head ringed by a poll of white feathers above a massive chest of white. In nature, its wingspan can reach 7½ feet. As depicted on the front of the Seal—or "obverse," to use the heraldic term—the eagle is displayed with wings open, holding in its beak a scroll with the *E Pluribus Unum* motto, while clutching an olive branch in one claw and a bundle of arrows in the other. When properly rendered, the eagle always faces toward the left.

With the adoption of the Great Seal, and the pride and prosperity of the young country, the boom in eagle

AMERICAN EAGLES / 31

Typographic eagles used for decorating posters, advertising broadsides and handbills were being sold to printers in the mid-19th Century by type foundries. Three portray the eagle clutching the traditional clusters of arrows and olive branches. But in one (top right) the bird rises phoenix-like from a nest of flames, while below it another has a nautical motif.

motifs truly began, creating an unending source of material for eagle collectors. Some of this material turns up in obvious places. But in my own experience, the eagles that give the most pleasure to the collector are those found by purest chance.

I discovered my favorite eagle one day while I was walking down Fifth Avenue in New York City. The 1939 World's Fair was going on at the time and, in the window of an opulent department store, I spotted a glorious 3-foot bird stamped in brass *(page 28)*. Used in the middle of the last century to decorate a speaker's platform during political campaigns, or to be carried in parades, this unusual object had five slots in the back to hold flagstaffs. Now it had been made part of a window display, and I wanted it.

As nonchalantly as possible, I made contact with the store's public relations representative and sounded out the possibility of buying the piece. It took several conversations before I managed to acquire it. Even today it seems to me a fine amalgamation of the many roles of the American eagle: patriotic emblem, piece of history and fine bit of craftsmanship.

MUSEUMS
Abby Aldrich Rockefeller Folk Art Center
Williamsburg, Virginia 23185

The Mariners Museum
Newport News, Virginia 23606

Mystic Seaport, Inc.
Mystic, Connecticut 06355

BOOKS
Herrick, Francis Hobart, *The American Eagle*. D. Appleton-Century Company, Inc., 1933. (Second edition, 1934.)

Hornung, Clarence P.:
The American Eagle in Art and Design.
Dover Publications, Inc., 1978.

Treasury of American Design, 2 vols. Harry N. Abrams, Inc., 1972.

Isaacson, Philip M., *The American Eagle*. New York Graphic Society, 1975.

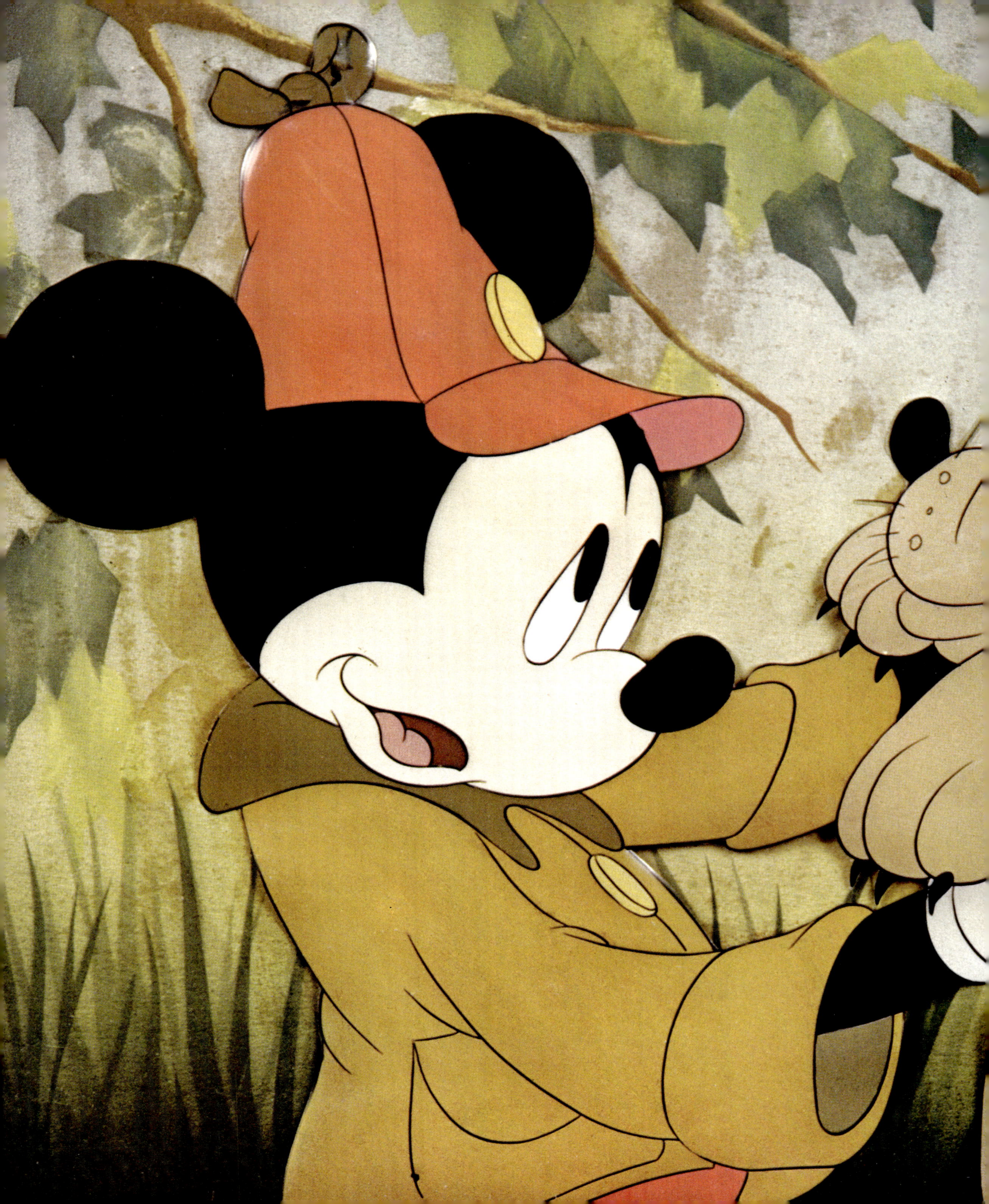

© Walt Disney Productions

Animation Film Art
The Reality of Fantasy

For anyone born in this century, a childhood without movie cartoons—Mickey Mouse, Betty Boop, Felix the Cat and their predecessors—would have been as unthinkable as a childhood without vaccination shots. The beloved cartoon characters racing and tumbling across the screen, bent upon mayhem and merrymaking, brought to life a fantasy world in which villainy was inevitably confounded and virtue always rewarded. Even children quickly learned that the fast-paced high jinks were created by photographing thousands of drawings onto movie film. This did not lessen their charm. On the contrary, for some devotees, myself included, the many bits and pieces of art work that made the cartoon fantasies possible were enjoyable in themselves, and became things to acquire and study.

Purely in terms of numbers, the animated film is a prodigious achievement. For a typical seven-minute in-

---

Robert Lesser, author of "A Celebration of Comic Art and Memorabilia," collects comical toys, dolls, premiums, and bubble-gum cards, as well as the original art for comic strips and film cartoons.

---

stallment of *Betty Boop*, as many as 120 artists were engaged in producing something like 30,000 drawings. For the first full-length animated film, Walt Disney's 1937 milestone, *Snow White and the Seven Dwarfs,* nearly a half million were required. And the total number of drawings made during the late 1930s and '40s, when production of animated films was at its height, must reach well into the millions.

Until the appearance of *Snow White,* most of this voluminous art work simply disappeared when the directors, cameramen and sound engineers were finished with it. Some of it was destroyed; some of it was carried home by the artists involved in its creation; some of it was casually given away as souvenirs to people who visited the studio. But Disney's sweet-faced heroine and

A rare "cel," with its original leafy background attached, shows closeups of Mickey Mouse and Pluto, two of Walt Disney's most popular creations, in a scene from "The Pointer."

34 / ANIMATION FILM ART

The panels above make up a section of a storyboard—an illustrated plot outline—for Raggedy Ann and Andy, produced by Fleischer Studios in 1940. The rough sketches, though splotched with ink, are still valuable. They are part of the collection of Woody Gellman.

A model sheet for Betty Boop is designed to standardize the style of all the artists working on the cartoon. It contains data on body proportions, dress, facial expressions and length of eyelashes, and even such details as Betty's flirtatious garter, which is "always on left leg."

ANIMATION FILM ART / 35

her retinue of personable dwarfs, greeted by public and critical acclaim, encouraged the studios to preserve the animators' art work and inspired the first serious impulse toward collecting it.

The man most responsible for recognizing animation film art as a potential collectible was an enterprising California art dealer named Guthrie Sayre Courvoisier. Shortly after *Snow White*'s release, Courvoisier approached Walt Disney Productions and suggested that there were sales possibilities in the "cels," or transparent sheets on which each bit of action in the film was set down (the word is short for "Celluloid," the material on which the art was once drawn). He foresaw a market for the cels among museums, school art departments, interior decorators and collectors of American art.

Courvoisier's prediction proved to be accurate. Although effects of the Great Depression still hampered sales of luxuries, the dealer reported that "without half trying," he had sold 65 cels for prices ranging from five dollars to $35. One cel, showing Snow White and animals looking through a window, had gone for $50. A few months later, the avant-garde Julien Levy Galleries in New York sold 63 cels in a single day.

From that day to this, the interest of collectors in animation film art has never abated. Fifteen hundred cels from the Beatles' 1968 movie, *Yellow Submarine,* sold out in 30 days, and the Disney studios found buyers for every one of the several hundred cels from the 1977 film, *The Rescuers,* that were released for sale. Disney even took to issuing reproductions of its most famous cels in limited-edition sets; in 1977 a set of four Snow White cels went for $1,200. And the studio was more than happy to buy back, sometimes at 10 or 20 times the purchase price, cels that it sold in the 1930s for $50.

Some contemporary collectors, like those of Courvoisier's day, look upon the cels as an art form and buy them as an investment, just as they would buy traditional forms of art. But many of the collectors are young people who buy the cels out of genuine affection for the cartoon characters they portray.

One New York City dealer in Disney memorabilia claims that most of his customers for cels are between 12 and 21 years old, and that they do not blink at paying several hundred dollars for a cel from a vintage Disney movie. He is often surprised at the lengths to which they will go when they have set their hearts on a particular cel. He once sold a $300 cel of Dopey to a teenager who arranged to pay for it in several installments, asking that

The woodland creatures that support the star of the motion picture "Bambi" are shown here painted on a clear plastic sheet, or cel, against a background painting.

36 / ANIMATION FILM ART

DANCE OF THE MUSHROOMS, FROM *FANTASIA*

The Animator as Fine Artist

Considered by many collectors to be the high point of animation film art, the feature-length movies of Walt Disney Productions contain some of the finest examples of the animator's skill. The components of the Disney style are economy of line, subtlety of coloring and an expressiveness that makes even animals seem human. All three characteristics can be seen in these cels from feature-length Disney films. These paintings, as well as the other Disney art in this article, are from the collection of Edward Deep and James Mondhank.

PINOCCHIO AND JIMINY CRICKET

SNOW WHITE

38 / ANIMATION FILM ART

A drawing from "Gertie," made in 1914, is one of only a few known to have survived from this early animated film.

Winsor McCay, Gertie's animator, traveled the vaudeville circuit with his film and appears in an insert on this advertising poster.

it be delivered to the home of a friend so that his mother would not find out about his purchase. Other customers, equally covetous, have made down payments from money that had been set aside for next month's rent, or have financed their purchases with elaborately complex payment schedules.

The focus of all this attention, the cel, is a piece of art work that is the culmination and centerpiece of a series of preliminary illustrations. The first step is the creation of a storyboard, a sequence of rough sketches outlining the action of the film. When the storyboard is approved, artists set to work painting the background scenes against which the action will take place. Because these will be used repeatedly, like the stage sets for a play, they are generally done on heavy paper or cardboard.

The characters are drawn separately, with each sheet showing the character in a slightly different position; all the sheets together register as motion when translated into film. From time to time in making these drawings, the artist may refer to another piece of art work, a model sheet, prepared by the studio to guide him in depicting a character's bodily proportions, facial expressions, or manner of moving or standing.

When the drawings are completed, they are traced onto the transparent plastic. The cels are then placed over the background scenes and photographed in sequence, one at a time, on movie film. When the film runs through the projector, the separate action drawings blend to create the illusion of motion.

All of this material is collectible—storyboards, background paintings, preliminary character drawings, model sheets, cels. One of my most prized possessions is a model sheet for Betty Boop *(page 34).* But the most popular collectibles, naturally, are the cels. This is partly because they are more numerous: there may be 50 cels for each of the background paintings. But cels are also popular because they are, in effect, portraits of the stars of the animated film. One particularly valuable collectible is a cel of the leading character—Betty Boop, Mickey Mouse, Popeye, Pinocchio—that is mounted on the original background.

The works of Walt Disney Productions and Fleischer Studios, both of which began producing animated films in the 1920s, are highly desirable. But the serious collectors also look for the work of the men who preceded them: the pioneers.

Experiments with animated drawings took place long before movies were invented, but the first animated film was produced in 1900 by an unknown artist employed by Thomas Edison's motion-picture company, and is now kept in the Library of Congress. This film, called *The Enchanted Drawing,* shows an artist sketching a sad-faced tramp on a drawing pad. As the artist lights a cigar in the tramp's mouth, the drawing impishly comes to life

ANIMATION FILM ART / 39

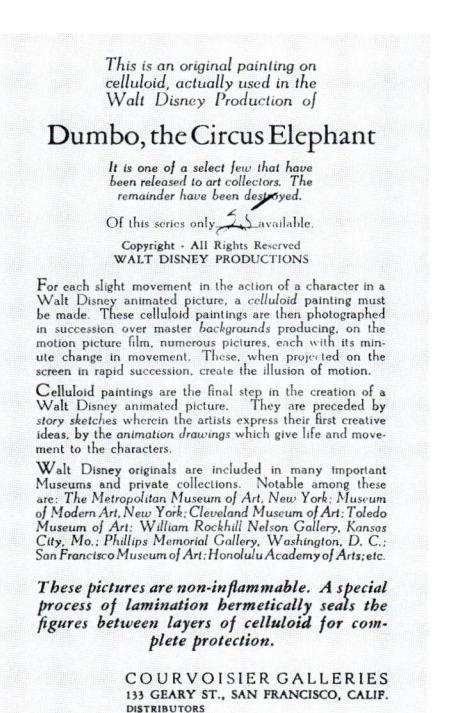

A cel from "Dumbo," accompanied by an authenticating certificate, was among those sold by Courvoisier Galleries of San Francisco in the 1940s, a move that established animation drawings as collectibles. Courvoisier's copywriter apparently confused his facts in the statement about safety in the bottom lines of the document. There was no fire hazard because the cels were made of nonflammable acetate. And even if the "protective" covering was flammable Celluloid—it probably was not—the danger was minimal.

and the tramp begins to puff out huge clouds of smoke, while the artist leaps back in feigned surprise.

Nine years later, New York newspaper cartoonist Winsor McCay, creator of a comic strip called Little Nemo, produced the first animated film that received wide public showing. McCay, a phenomenally fast artist, won a bet with fellow artists who challenged him to produce the 4,000 drawings needed for a five-minute film based on Little Nemo.

A showman as well as an artist, McCay took his animated film on a vaudeville tour. His act was so well received that he went back to the drawing board to produce *The Story of the Mosquito,* released in 1912, *Gertie the Dinosaur,* in 1914, and *The Sinking of the Lusitania,* in 1916. During the making of the latter film, he discovered he could substitute Celluloid for rice paper and reuse a single background for a number of frames. The result was an enormous saving in production time.

McCay always acted as the master of ceremonies in presenting his films to the audience. The first animator who sent his films out on their own, so to speak, was J. R. Bray, creator of the *Colonel Heeza Liar* series, which began in 1913. Bray's studio was the training ground for some of the most famous names in animated film. One of his animators was Walter Lantz, who later created Woody Woodpecker, and among his directors were Paul Terry, Max Fleischer and Earl Hurd. Terry subsequently produced *Terrytoons,* and Fleischer was responsible for *Betty Boop.* Hurd, who produced *Bobby Bumps* for Bray, is actually best known for his invention, with Bray, of a system of pins and sprocket holes for aligning cels and background during photography.

The growing popularity of animated films introduced a growing roster of cartoon characters: in the 1920s Mutt and Jeff, Krazy Kat, the Katzenjammer Kids, Maggie and Jiggs from *Bringing Up Father,* and finally, Mickey Mouse. Mickey was joined by other Disney favorites—Donald Duck, Goofy and Pluto. Warner Brothers brought out *Looney Tunes* and *Merrie Melodies,* and created many characters whose names became household words: Porky Pig, Daffy Duck, Bugs Bunny and Roadrunner. Metro-Goldwyn-Mayer offered the relentless battles of Tom and Jerry, while United Productions of America created dim-sighted Mister Magoo.

The men who drew these cartoon favorites are often the subject of serious study by critics and collectors. In 1975, for example, the Museum of Modern Art in New York presented a retrospective exhibition of the work of Charles "Chuck" Jones, the originator of Roadrunner. But in the view of most experts, the highest level of

40 / ANIMATION FILM ART

Reincarnated Classics

Collectors occasionally come across colored cels, apparently from old cartoons that were originally produced in black and white. This seemingly contradictory situation is simply explained: the old cartoons are being readied for reruns on television. The owners of such oldies as *Betty Boop (right)* and *Porky Pig (below)* have copies of their films reanimated in color. The films are projected a frame at a time so that the images can be traced to outline new background and character cels, which are then colored.

BETTY BOOP AND VILLAIN

PORKY PIG AND BULLY

animation film art was achieved by Disney in five full-length feature films produced before and during World War II: *Pinocchio, Fantasia, Dumbo, Bambi,* and above all, *Snow White,* for which cost was almost ignored in a search for flawless detail.

My own involvement in animation film art grew out of an interest in tracking down source material on a subject, any subject: I was trained to be a bibliographer. One day in the 1960s, sitting with fellow alumni at the University of Chicago, I was challenged half-jokingly to compile a history of the cartoon that appeared on the face of the Mickey Mouse watch I had bought on a whim a few days before.

Intrigued, I set out to do just that. My research led me to museums, galleries, out-of-the-way antique markets and the archives of Hollywood studios. From that, I progressed to collecting the materials on which my research was based. Examples of film art were then easier to buy than they are today; in the 1960s, interest in the medium had not reached current proportions. I managed to acquire cheaply a number of beautiful items, including my Betty Boop model sheet. But I guess my favorite is a cel from Disney's *Mother Goose Goes to Hollywood,* a 1937 feature-length film that combined animated-film characters with real people. The cel depicts then-popular radio comedian Joe Penner—famous for the line, "Wanna buy a duck?"—carrying Donald Duck in a roasting pan toward an oven.

In acquiring my collection, I found that museums are a good place to learn about animation film art. Several museums across the country have collections *(box, right).* But it is often worth inquiring about film art at any museum that specializes in 20th Century art, on the chance that it may have some examples of animation art work tucked away in storage. Sometimes the curatorial staffs of these museums can be helpful in directing collectors toward local sources.

There are also dealers who specialize in animated-cartoon art, such as the Gallery Lainzburg in Cedar Rapids, Iowa, and the Circle Galleries in San Francisco, Chicago and New York. And the comic-book conventions held periodically in most major cities are usually attended by a few fans of animated cartoons who are willing to discuss buying, selling and trading—as well as to exchange information.

Any collectible associated with animated film—storyboard, model sheets, backgrounds—requires some care. But the most popular item, the cels themselves, may need very special handling since most cels made prior to 1951 were of Celluloid (cellulose nitrate), a flammable material that decomposes spontaneously and can pose a serious fire hazard in storage. Less combustible cellulose acetate began to be used before World War II and came into general use after 1951; it is the same material used for home-movie film and is perfectly safe to store at home. A few cels of cellulose nitrate, framed and hanging on a wall, are not a serious fire danger. But a drawer full of nitrate cels can indeed be dangerous. If you are lucky enough to acquire more than a few nitrate cels, store them individually without any combustible wrappings in closed metal containers, and keep the containers in a cool, well-ventilated place. Cool temperatures and ventilation are necessary even if there is no particular fire hazard. Unless conditions are kept within normal limits, nitrate cels may melt. Veteran animators recall with chagrin the loss of valuable cels that, stacked together, simply fused into indistinguishable lumps.

Cels are also perishable because their paint tends to flake; to make the paint adhere, it has to be laid on heavily. The best method of preventing flaking is to mount the cels between two layers of glass. A glass mounting also disposes of the problems that can be raised when cels are displayed against a cardboard backing, or within a cardboard mat or frame. If you do decide to mat or mount a cel against cardboard, be sure the cardboard is the kind, available in most art-supply stores, that is made of 100 per cent rag stock and free of acid; otherwise it may discolor the cel. And whatever the mounting material, display the cel in a spot where it will not be exposed to heat or humidity.

For related material see the article on Comics in a separate volume of this encyclopedia.

MUSEUMS
Baltimore Museum of Art
Baltimore, Maryland 21218

Museum of Modern Art
New York, New York 10019

COLLECTORS ORGANIZATIONS
ASIFA, International Animated Film Society
1680 North Vine
Hollywood, California 90028

BOOKS
Cabarga, Leslie, *The Fleischer Story.* Crown Publishers, Inc., 1976.

Finch, Christopher, *The Art of Walt Disney.* Harry N. Abrams, Inc., 1973.

Madsen, Roy, *Animated Film: Concepts, Methods, Uses.* Interland Publishing, Inc., 1969.

Maltin, Leonard, *Disney Films.* Crown Publishers, Inc., 1972.

Arrowheads
Discovering Prehistoric America

Almost anywhere in America, anyone who keeps his eyes sharp and knows where to look and what to look for can find Indian arrowheads. A man I know picked up 35 perfect examples in an hour in Franklin County, Ohio. And a young Midwestern couple collected 125 in three hours.

Most of the implements they found were not really arrowheads at all—the bow appeared in the New World only in about 500 A.D.; they were spear points, knife blades and various cutting tools. Together they tell a fascinating story of the peoples that populated America

Lar Hothem gave up a sporting-goods business to devote himself fulltime to Indian artifacts. He writes about them as well as collecting them, and is a past president of the Columbus, Ohio, Writer's Club.

before Columbus. From their forms can be deduced much about the way prehistoric Indians hunted, fought, built houses, and made the things they needed. In my own collection, gathered in Ohio and nearby states, I have points—or arrowheads—spanning a period of 12,000 years. Some of them are small, true arrowheads, probably no more than 1,500 years old. But the bulk of my collection, more than 80 per cent of it, consists of points that were affixed to spears or lances. These were hurled by hand or with the aid of a spear thrower, a device called an atlatl, and they are thought to have been the predominant weapon used through much of the country's prehistory *(chart, pages 44-45).*

The oldest of these points, called Paleo-Indian, are also the largest. They are 3 inches or more in length, and are often fluted, or channeled, down the middle to receive the lance shaft. They appear to have been made before 8000 B.C. by people who hunted for big game—bison and mammoths—and who needed weapons heavy enough to bring down their massive prey. The next-oldest points, called Archaic, date from 8000 B.C. to around 1000 B.C. and are generally either notched or stemmed at the base, a refinement that made them

Two very early spear points, from a period called Paleo-Indian, differ mostly in the handling of the base. The point on the right is slightly indented to hold the shaft more securely.

Four different kinds of flint were used to fashion these prehistoric Midwestern spear points. The large black point, 3 inches long, is a Clovis type, identified by its grooved, or fluted, base. Clovis-type points were made by many of the earliest prehistoric peoples.

The author examines a lancehead that he spotted during a walk-and-poke search through a plowed field in central Ohio. One of his most important pieces of equipment is the long pole, which he uses as a tool to dislodge half-buried finds.

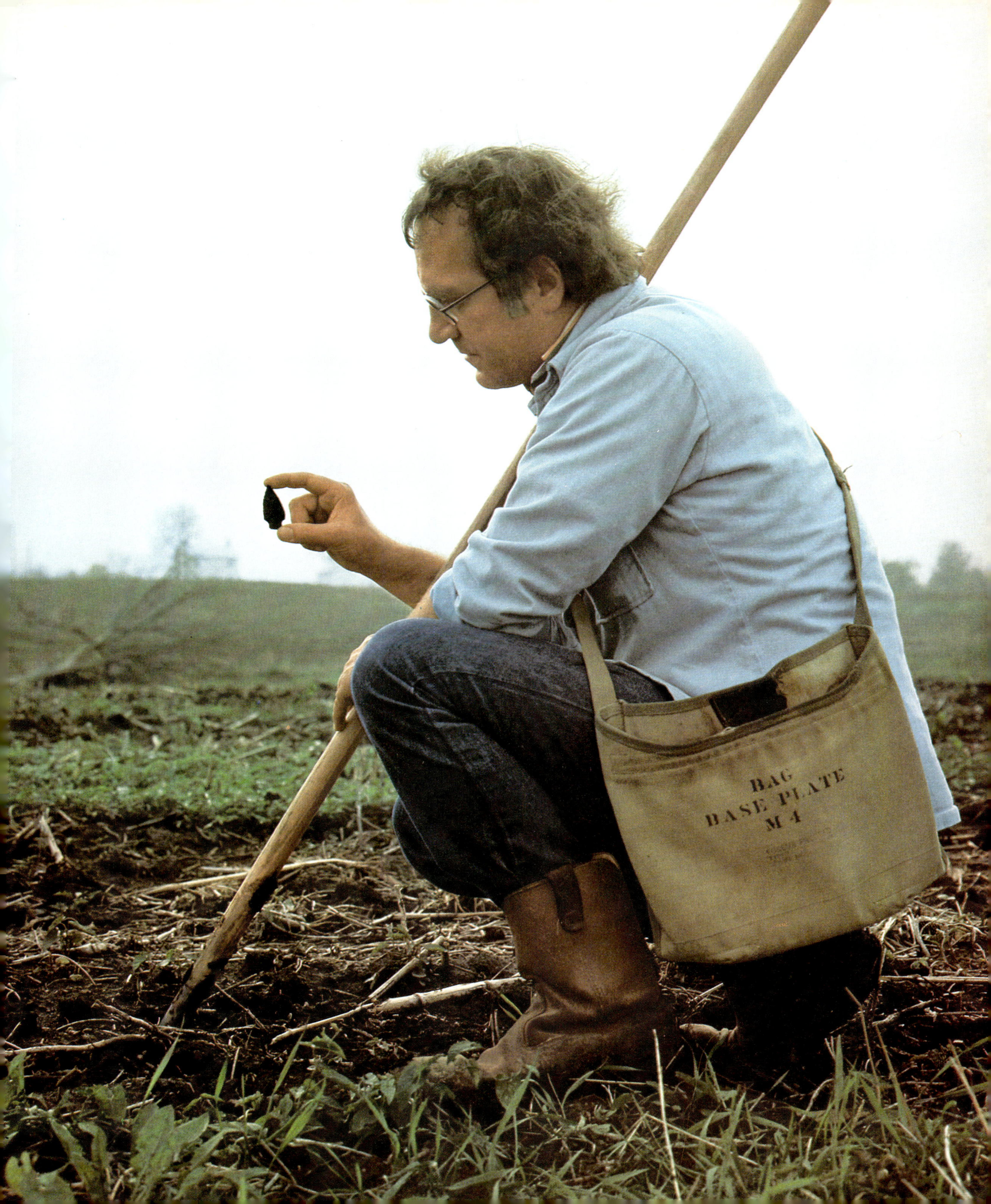
BAG
BASE PLATE
M 4

44 / ARROWHEADS

A TIMETABLE FOR POINT MANUFACTURE

Prehistoric projectile points found in the continental United States are generally divided into four main periods: Paleo-Indian, Archaic, Middle and Late. In some parts of the country the Middle and Late periods are named for the predominant regional culture—the Middle and Late periods in the Northeast are called Woodland.

Not every section of the country passed through all four periods, and the chronological dates for each period vary from region to region. The Paleo-Indian period, for example, apparently occurred in the Northwest at about 12,000 B.C., but did not rise in the Southeast until 8000 B.C. Similarly, though the technology of point making advanced in each period in certain characteristic ways (drawings, opposite), there were many regional differences. The chart on these pages describes points for most periods under regional headings to help collectors hazard a guess about the age of their finds.

		SIZE OF POINTS	SHAPE	MATERIAL
NORTHEAST				
PALEO-INDIAN	10,000-8000 B.C.	1½" to 5"	Fluted bases	Flint
ARCHAIC	8000-1000 B.C.	2" to 4"	Notched bases	Quartzite, flint, slate, copper
EARLY WOODLAND	1000 B.C.-200 A.D.	1½" to 2"	Side-notched, stemmed, corner-notched	Quartzite, flint, slate
MIDDLE WOODLAND	200-1200 A.D.	1½" to 2"	Stemmed, notched bases	Quartzite, flint, slate
LATE WOODLAND	1200-1600 A.D.	1" to 1½"	Triangular, narrow types; stemmed and notched types; diamond-shaped	Quartzite, flint, slate, antler, split bone
SOUTHEAST				
PALEO-INDIAN	8000-6000 B.C.	1½" to 5"	Fluted bases	Flint
ARCHAIC	6000-1000 B.C.	1½" to 3"	Bifurcated bases, serrated or beveled edges	Flint, quartzite
WOODLAND	1000 B.C.-1000 A.D.	1" to 2"	Stemmed and notched, thick	Flint, quartzite, quartz
MISSISSIPPIAN	1000-1500 A.D.	1" to 1½"	Triangular, unstemmed, side-notched	Flint, quartzite, quartz
UPPER GREAT LAKES REGION (Minnesota, Wisconsin and Michigan)				
EARLY PALEO-INDIAN	11,000-7000 B.C.	2" to 4"	Fluted bases	Flint, quartzite
LATE PALEO-INDIAN	7000-5000 B.C.	3" to 6"	Stemmed	Flint, quartzite, taconite, argillite
ARCHAIC	5000-500 B.C.	1" to 3"	Socketed, spiked bases; corner- and side-notched; stemmed and unstemmed	Beaten copper, flint
EARLY WOODLAND	500 B.C.-500 A.D.	1½" to 3"	Broad and flat, wide stems	Quartz, flint, some copper
MIDDLE WOODLAND	500-1200 A.D.	1½" to 3"	Wide, thin with rounded notches	Quartz, flint
LATE WOODLAND	1200-1600 A.D.	1" to 1½"	Side- or corner-notched, but some triangular with neither stems nor notches	Quartz, flint
MIDWEST				
EARLY PALEO-INDIAN	To 10,000 B.C.	5" to 6"	Fluted bases	High-quality flint
LATE PALEO-INDIAN	10,000-8000 B.C.	3" to 5"	Slim, fluted and unfluted, short-stemmed bases	Flint
ARCHAIC	8000-1000 B.C.	¾" to 4"	Stemmed and side-notched, with bifurcated bases, serrated edges	Flint
EARLY WOODLAND	1000-100 B.C.	3"	Most common is Adena, a sturdy point with long straight stems and sharp shoulders	Flint
MIDDLE WOODLAND	100 B.C.-700 A.D.	2" to 3"	Most common is Hopewell, similar to Adena (*above*) but smaller and corner-notched	Flint, some obsidian
LATE WOODLAND	700-1200 A.D.	1½"	Thin points, triangular shape	Flint
MISSISSIPPIAN	1200-1650 A.D.	¾" to 1½"	Notched and stemmed; others triangular without notches or stems	Flint

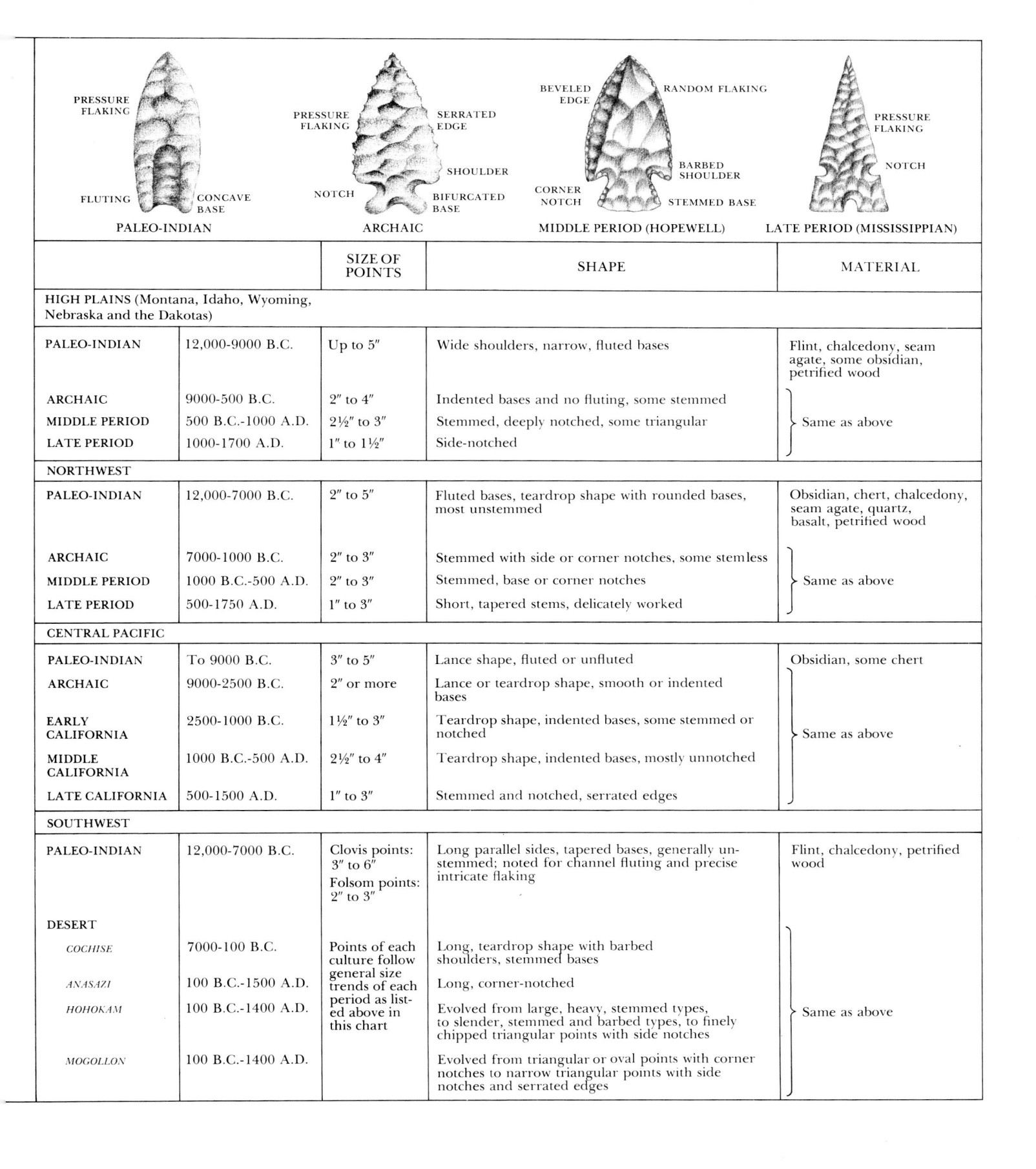

Arrowhead Types

PALEO-INDIAN: Pressure Flaking, Fluting, Concave Base

ARCHAIC: Pressure Flaking, Serrated Edge, Shoulder, Notch, Bifurcated Base

MIDDLE PERIOD (HOPEWELL): Beveled Edge, Random Flaking, Barbed Shoulder, Corner Notch, Stemmed Base

LATE PERIOD (MISSISSIPPIAN): Pressure Flaking, Notch

		SIZE OF POINTS	SHAPE	MATERIAL
HIGH PLAINS (Montana, Idaho, Wyoming, Nebraska and the Dakotas)				
PALEO-INDIAN	12,000-9000 B.C.	Up to 5"	Wide shoulders, narrow, fluted bases	Flint, chalcedony, seam agate, some obsidian, petrified wood
ARCHAIC	9000-500 B.C.	2" to 4"	Indented bases and no fluting, some stemmed	Same as above
MIDDLE PERIOD	500 B.C.-1000 A.D.	2½" to 3"	Stemmed, deeply notched, some triangular	Same as above
LATE PERIOD	1000-1700 A.D.	1" to 1½"	Side-notched	Same as above
NORTHWEST				
PALEO-INDIAN	12,000-7000 B.C.	2" to 5"	Fluted bases, teardrop shape with rounded bases, most unstemmed	Obsidian, chert, chalcedony, seam agate, quartz, basalt, petrified wood
ARCHAIC	7000-1000 B.C.	2" to 3"	Stemmed with side or corner notches, some stemless	Same as above
MIDDLE PERIOD	1000 B.C.-500 A.D.	2" to 3"	Stemmed, base or corner notches	Same as above
LATE PERIOD	500-1750 A.D.	1" to 3"	Short, tapered stems, delicately worked	Same as above
CENTRAL PACIFIC				
PALEO-INDIAN	To 9000 B.C.	3" to 5"	Lance shape, fluted or unfluted	Obsidian, some chert
ARCHAIC	9000-2500 B.C.	2" or more	Lance or teardrop shape, smooth or indented bases	Same as above
EARLY CALIFORNIA	2500-1000 B.C.	1½" to 3"	Teardrop shape, indented bases, some stemmed or notched	Same as above
MIDDLE CALIFORNIA	1000 B.C.-500 A.D.	2½" to 4"	Teardrop shape, indented bases, mostly unnotched	Same as above
LATE CALIFORNIA	500-1500 A.D.	1" to 3"	Stemmed and notched, serrated edges	Same as above
SOUTHWEST				
PALEO-INDIAN	12,000-7000 B.C.	Clovis points: 3" to 6" Folsom points: 2" to 3"	Long parallel sides, tapered bases, generally unstemmed; noted for channel fluting and precise intricate flaking	Flint, chalcedony, petrified wood
DESERT		Points of each culture follow general size trends of each period as listed above in this chart		
COCHISE	7000-100 B.C.		Long, teardrop shape with barbed shoulders, stemmed bases	Same as above
ANASAZI	100 B.C.-1500 A.D.		Long, corner-notched	Same as above
HOHOKAM	100 B.C.-1400 A.D.		Evolved from large, heavy, stemmed types, to slender, stemmed and barbed types, to finely chipped triangular points with side notches	Same as above
MOGOLLON	100 B.C.-1400 A.D.		Evolved from triangular or oval points with corner notches to narrow triangular points with side notches and serrated edges	Same as above

46 / ARROWHEADS

easier to fasten securely to the shaft. They were used to hunt smaller game by people who also fished and foraged for a good part of their diet.

In the period that followed, called the Middle period, the bow and arrow were introduced and points became smaller. By this time people had begun to settle in villages and had developed distinctive local styles of working in stone. Consequently, points became identified with specific cultures, such as Woodland or Desert. They also tended to change more rapidly in design. Thus, the Woodland points of the Northeast passed through four distinct phases—generally designated early, middle, late and final Woodland.

The Middle period ends around 1200 A.D. and is followed by the last or Late period, 1200 to 1600 or 1700, during which points became very small indeed. Some are barely an inch long. In many cultures Late period points are very sophisticated. Mississippian points, for example, which are found throughout the Midwest, are triangular or side-notched, without stems, and may have been designed to slip from the shaft when it was withdrawn from the body of the animal (or person), leaving a particularly painful wound.

Wherever there are arrowheads and spear points there are usually related chipped artifacts. Some were apparently used as knives or daggers, or as scrapers for cleaning animal hides. Most scrapers are quartz flakes, an inch or two long, with beveled or sharply angled working edges along one or both sides. Knives and daggers are longer, with one or two cutting sides, and may have a serrated or saw-toothed edge. Some have

These five heavy-duty points, 2 to 4 inches long, are thick in cross section and have sturdy bases, but the edges are thin and well formed. All of them belong to a prehistoric period called Archaic.

A collection of points with bifurcated, or double-lobed, bases shows a considerable range in shape and size—2 to 5 inches. Designed to slip into a cleft shaft, bifurcated points fitted very securely.

Side-notched points had a variety of uses in prehistoric cultures. The unusually large specimen in the middle of the top row, 2½ inches long, has serrated edges and was probably created for cutting.

Bevel-edged points with their chisel-like cutting surface are believed to have been used for butchering. They were often resharpened until they became very short. The largest above is nearly 4 inches long.

ARROWHEADS / 47

Dovetail points, which have curving sides and deeply notched bases, are admired by collectors for their symmetry, and because they are usually well made from fine flint. The largest point at left is 3 inches long.

Points from recent archeological periods, such as these made by Hopewell and other Woodland-era Indians, frequently have broad bases and shallow notches for attaching to a shaft. The Hopewell Indians often buried points like these in the elaborate, dome-shaped mounds that held their dead.

All but one of the points at left are considered true arrowheads, designed to be shot from bows. The one exception may be the small point in the center of the bottom row, which could be a lancehead. None of these points is more than 1¼ inches long, and all have distinctive shoulders and bases.

These flint points, from a central Ohio site, range from about 1,500 to 6,000 years old. The two smallest are probably true arrowheads. The rest evidently were lance points—except the round-bladed tool (top right), which was probably a scraper for cleaning hides.

straight or rounded bases; others are notched or stemmed for fastening to a handle of wood, bone or antler *(drawing, page 45)*.

Other specialized tools sometimes found with points and blades are drills, perforators, gravers and hammerstones. Drills were designed to make holes in stone, slate or wood, and are long and slender, averaging between 1 and 3 inches. Some have T-shaped tops and may have been fitted to a wooden shaft that was turned by a bow or a similar device to bore holes. Because of the drills' delicate construction, they are almost never found in one piece. Perforators also made holes, but in hides rather than in heavier materials. They resemble drills but are shorter, an inch or less, and sturdier. Often the base is thick, for grasping with the fingers. Gravers, used for cutting bone, antlers and hides, and for incising marks on those materials, have a short, razor-sharp edge, while the ball-shaped hammerstone, literally a tool-making tool, was used to reduce blocks of stone to thinner, more manageable sizes. These stone blanks were then shaped into the desired configuration by a process called percussion flaking: the stone was struck with an antler club or another stone. Then the edge was created by pressure flaking, the carefully controlled removal of smaller flakes.

But of all these kinds of artifacts, the ones found most frequently, and therefore most often collected, are the points. They also occur in the greatest variety. In the

ARROWHEADS / 49

A collection of true arrowheads in triangular forms probably dates to the most recent prehistoric period, called Mississippian. Light and thin, they were easy to produce, and were manufactured by the thousands for use in both hunting and warfare.

continental United States alone archeologists recognize more than 400 distinct types. They are distinguished by region, by material, by shape and by the distinctive pattern in which they are flaked.

In central Ohio, where I live, points were almost always made of flint, and in fact at least 10 different kinds of flint were quarried there. Just 30 miles from my home is one quarry, called Flintridge, which produced a particularly handsome, multihued, translucent stone. But in other parts of the country, points were often made of materials other than flint. Indians of the Northeast coast used slate and a kind of quartz called sugar because it is white. In the western Great Lakes region, points of copper, bone and deer antler have been found, and in the Plains states and the Southwest you can find points of a volcanic glass called obsidian, and of petrified wood. Obsidian points also turn up on the West Coast, but there the Indians also made points of chert, which resembles flint but is usually of lower quality. And the Northwest coast is famous for its long, delicately worked "gem points" of agate and chalcedony, two translucent varieties of quartz.

Every collector of these artifacts has his own favorite method of operating. I find most of my points by what is termed surface hunting, a simple walk-and-look method. One place I often head for is the shoreline of reservoirs behind major dams, where the lapping water often loosens buried material and carries it to the water's

Three of the four major periods of point manufacture are probably represented above. Most collectors classify the largest point, 3 inches long, as Paleo-Indian, the oldest period. The others are Archaic and Woodland, as indicated by their size and the design of the base.

Varied notching styles give the shoulders, barbs and stems of these flint points different silhouettes. They are 1½ to 4 inches long, and are rated highly by collectors because the flint is of good quality.

Two small true arrowheads (top row, center), and a heavy-duty blade with an intricate, serrated edge (bottom row, second from left), are included in these points, which range from 1,500 to 6,000 years old.

edge. Once, after a nonproductive afternoon of field hunting, I headed home by way of a local reservoir and was pleased to note that the water level was 8 feet below normal. In less than an hour I found nine perfect points and twice as many broken ones.

But my real happy hunting ground is farm land, especially newly turned farm land after the kind of heavy rain that arrowhead collectors call a point-washer. I have my best luck on higher ground or beside water, the locations preferred by prehistoric peoples for their settlements. And I do my most intense looking in the spring, when the farmers have begun to work their fields but before the crops are up. Most farmers will permit you to hunt at this time if you explain what you are seeking, and some will even allow you to walk through the fields when the corn and soybeans are up, but still small. You must always ask permission, however, before you hunt over any private land.

If a site is new to me, I begin by walking and looking at random until I strike what appears to be a productive zone. I look for the glint of flint chips, evidence of prehistoric occupation—and almost inevitably where I find chips I find points close by. Then I become more systematic. I walk in straight parallel lines, about 10 feet apart, and in a direction that puts the sun neither directly in my eyes nor directly behind me, so that I am not walking in my own shadow. I also carry a long, stout pole to use for poking at exposed pieces of flint (and for discouraging unfriendly dogs). The poking is necessary because points are seldom completely out of the earth. Any collector has a favorite story of the tiny bit of exposed flint that quickly led him to a superb find.

But mine is not the only way to find points. In Florida, collectors often don scuba-diving gear to search springs

Fresh breaks on the tip and right-hand side of this side-notched point, and on the left-hand side of the base, mark it as having been damaged recently by farm equipment.

These points, made by the Adenans, a relatively late Midwestern culture, are sometimes mistaken by novices for points from the earlier Archaic period because of similar traits, like heavy-stemmed bases.

and streams near early habitation sites. And in parts of the West where vegetation is thin, dust storms are a boon to collectors. Walking through a "blow-out," a depression created by wind, they can quickly fill their pockets with fine points of many kinds. Also in many parts of the West and Northwest, collectors hunt points much as prospectors panned for gold—by sifting the soil through wire-mesh screens. Two especially popular places for screening are along riverbanks and at the mouths of rivers where the ground is sandy and where there are many Indian sites. But never try to dig for points in the manner of archeologists; it will probably be illegal. Federal and state legislation now prohibits amateur digging on most major prehistoric sites.

These techniques for surface hunting not only increase your chance of turning up artifacts but also help you to find the more valuable ones. There are six generally accepted criteria that determine the value of points to collectors.

One is size. A large point is usually more desirable than a small one, not only because it makes a splendid showing, but also because it is rare. Even though flint is extremely hard, it is also quite brittle, and few large points survive unmarred, especially if they happen to have been in a field that has been heavily cultivated for many years. Consequently, large points are scarce, and scarcity enhances their value.

Another criterion is material. Flint and other chippable substances come in many grades of quality, ranging from dull to near-gemstone. The finer the quality of the material, the higher the value.

A third is balance: how symmetrical is the point? Draw an imaginary line from the tip to the center of the base and compare the two halves. The more they resemble each other, the better the balance and again, the greater the point's worth.

The fourth criterion is work style, a very important consideration. This covers not only the finished appearance of the point, but also the manner in which the artisan fashioned it. It includes chipping patterns, which can range from random flaking, in which the flake scars are large and irregular, to flaking that runs in neat parallel lines across the surface of the point, sometimes horizontally, sometimes obliquely, sometimes in chevron stripes. It also includes the care with which the notches, edges and tip are formed, and the amount of fine detail work involved, such as basal grinding.

The fifth criterion is condition. A damaged point is less valuable than a perfect one. Even as little as ¼ inch broken off the tip or shoulder of an otherwise splendid specimen can sharply lower its value.

Finally, value depends on a handful of attributes mostly involving esthetics: a point's size, condition, age, rarity or simply that it is pleasing. The point is also

52 / ARROWHEADS

Snub-nosed end scrapers, believed to have been used to prepare hides, are often found in perfect condition because of their compact construction. They are almost identical through all North American time periods and in all locations. The rounded end was the working edge.

The knives above, ranging from 3 to 5 inches long, come from different prehistoric periods. The chalcedony knife (bottom left), slender and brittle, astonishingly turned up intact in a much-plowed field.

These triangular points, probably used as knives, are 2 and 5 inches long. Both may have originally been hafted for easier control. The small knife is of especially fine translucent flint.

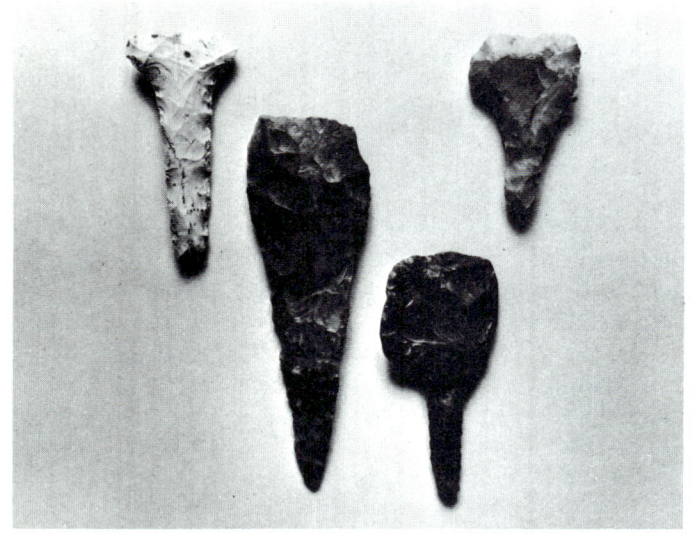

Flint drills with their slender points are common finds on the sites of prehistoric villages, where they were used to make holes in stone, slate or wood. The largest of these is nearly 3 inches long.

Except for the large double-tipped point from about 4000 B.C., the age of these artifacts is uncertain. To some degree, so are their uses. Most unusual is the ornament resembling a human profile (top).

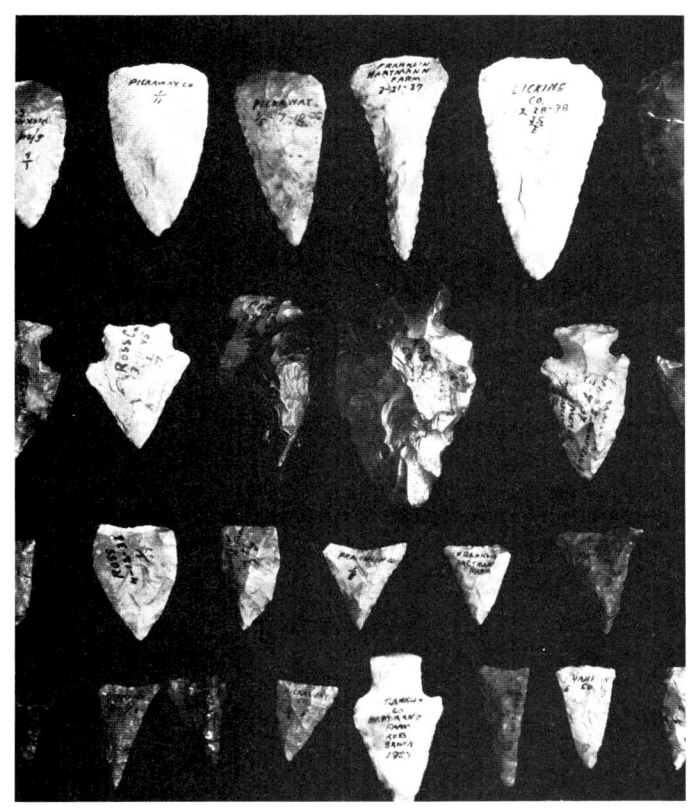

A collection of prehistoric Indian artifacts purchased by the author includes blades, drills, spear points and arrowheads. The India-ink notations specify the date and place of discovery.

prized if the stone is glossy, translucent or beautifully colored—in either one color or a mixture of several.

One vital factor not covered in this list of criteria for gauging worth is authenticity. This is a growing problem. A well-known collector once confided privately to a group of friends that several of the better points and blades he had acquired were, upon close examination, probably fake. I have heard people say you can tell a fake by the clumsiness of the chipping; that no one today can chip as well as the ancients did. Not so. There are modern chippers who can duplicate every technique used in prehistoric America, and do it convincingly. Fakes, however, tend to fall into two categories: copies of points that are rare, or of points that are large and showy. And they are invariably perfect in every detail.

One way to avoid fakes is to know your source. Reputable dealers may offer reproductions, but they will tell you so. Another good way to be sure of authenticity is to purchase points offered at meetings of amateur archeological societies *(box, right)*. Some of these societies are so scrupulous that they have committees to screen their points to be sure they are genuine. Many of them also publish material that can be extremely helpful for learning about local flints and chipping styles. In fact, they are often a fascinating source of information on a region's prehistory and what is being done to preserve it. Collecting arrowheads is of course part of that preservation—and of all the satisfactions of collecting them, that may be the most satisfying of all.

For related material, see the articles on Baskets, Beads, Knives and Navajo Blankets in separate volumes of The Encyclopedia of Collectibles.

MUSEUMS
Most state, county and municipal museums have significant collections of local Indian artifacts, and there are in addition many local private museums that charge admission. Chambers of Commerce can often provide names and addresses.

Field Museum of Natural History
Chicago, Illinois 60605

Museum of the American Indian
New York, New York 10032

National Museum of Natural History
Smithsonian Institution
Washington, D.C. 20560

COLLECTORS ORGANIZATIONS
The Central States Archaeological Societies, Inc.
6118 Scott Street
Davenport, Iowa 52806

Eastern States Archaeological Federation
RD #2, Box 166
Dover, Delaware 19901

Ohio Archaeological Society
35 West Riverglen Drive
Columbus, Ohio 43085

Oregon Archaeological Society
P.O. Box 13293
Portland, Oregon 97213

BOOKS
Bell, Robert E., and Perino, Gregory, *Guide to the Identification of Certain American Indian Projectile Points.* Special Bulletins No. 1-4, Oklahoma Anthropological Society, 1958-1971.

Ceram, C. W., *The First American.* Harcourt Brace Jovanovich Inc., 1971.

Miles, Charles, *Indian and Eskimo Artifacts of North America.* Henry Regnery Company, 1963.

Vanburen, G. E., *Arrowheads and Projectile Points.* Arrowhead Publishing Co., 1974.

Willey, Gordon R., *An Introduction to American Archaeology, Vol. 1: North and Middle America.* Prentice-Hall, Inc., 1966.

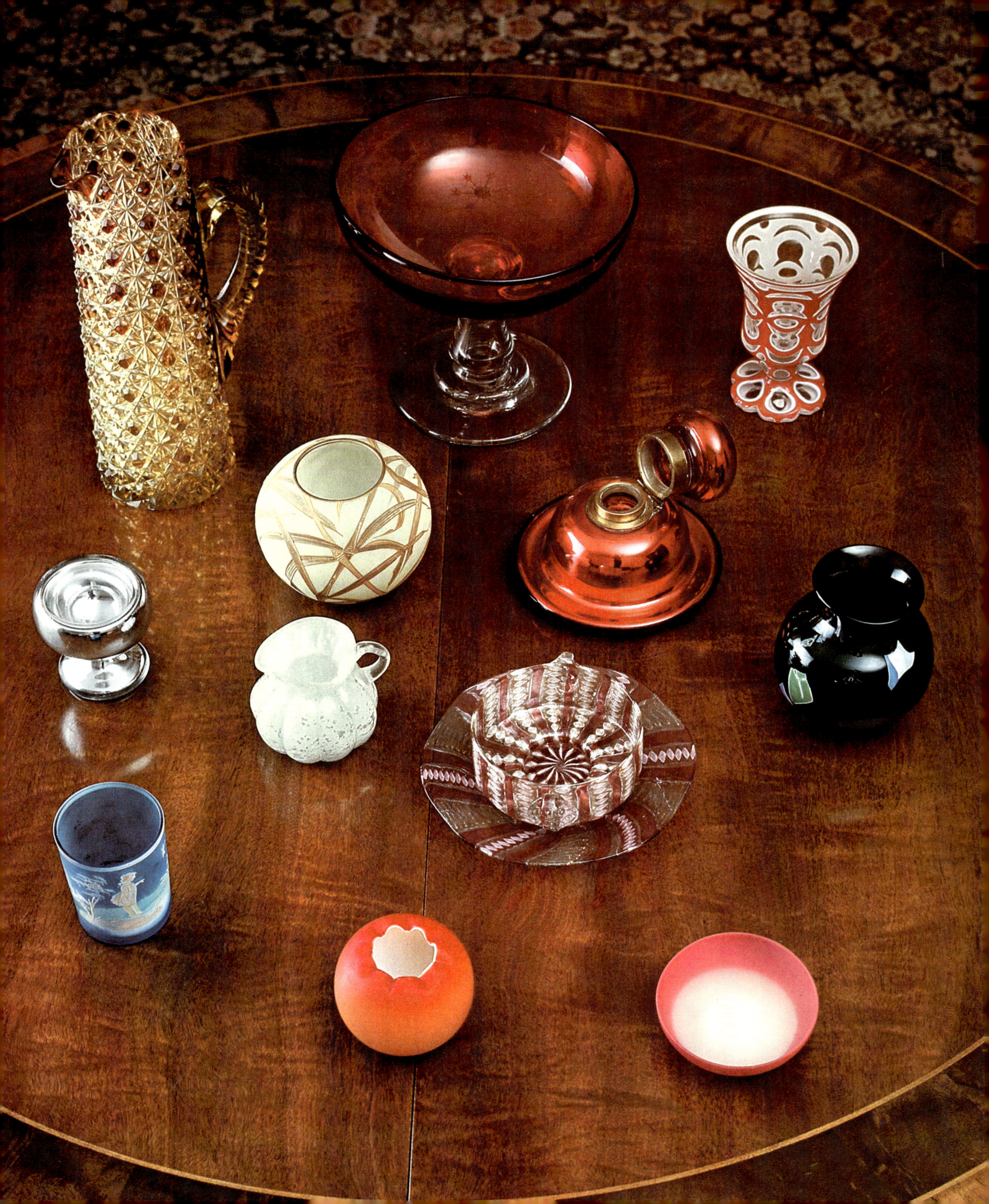

Art Glass
Victorians' Fanciful Ware

During the last quarter of the 19th Century, American glass manufacturers created some of the most colorful, whimsical and charming glassware ever made. It was called art glass, and it was made for well-to-do Victorians, whose taste for gingerbread and bric-a-brac was matched only by their desire to possess the latest thing in lemonade pitchers, toothpick holders, sauce dishes, flower vases, candy baskets, finger bowls, inkwells, tumblers, goblets, creamers and compotes. To satisfy the demand for this glass, more than two dozen kinds were created, most of them between 1880 and 1900.

Although almost all of the popular American art glass was hand blown and hand decorated, it was paradoxical-

---

Dorothy-Lee Jones has collected glass since childhood. Parts of her collection frequently appear in loan exhibits at museums, and she has served as president of the National Early American Glass Club.

---

ly produced and sold by commercial glass companies whose bread-and-butter products were bottles and window glass. There were fewer than a dozen of these firms; all of them saw art glass as a means of stabilizing their businesses and broadening their markets. Nearly all were in the East, around Boston, or in the Midwest—Ohio, West Virginia and western Pennsylvania—where costs, especially for fuel, were cheaper.

Although the techniques and chemistry used in making art glass had been known in Europe since the early 19th Century, they did not influence the American glass industry until the 1850s, when many talented British and Bohemian glassmakers emigrated to America. Bohemian craftsmen were the crucial factor, since they

In this assemblage of art glass are, in the outer circle, clockwise from top left: a lemonade pitcher in Amberina, a shaded glass; a ruby compote; a pink-and-white layered glass; a black glass vase containing lava; and two examples of a shaded glass called Peach Blow. The tumbler decorated with white figurines is Mary Gregory glass—named for a woman who painted such figures—and the shiny salt dish is Silvered glass. In the inner circle, from upper left, are an opal bowl with enameled leaves; a red Silvered-glass inkwell; a lattice-patterned finger bowl; and a metal-spangled creamer.

An Amberina flower-shaped vase with a globular pistil rests on a mirror. Like all Amberina glass, its shading is created by heat.

This stork vase is a rare example of one kind of art glass that was not hand blown: Amberina pressed glass. It was made around 1884.

55

A GUIDE TO TYPES OF ART GLASS

AGATA: Imitates the mottled appearance of agate. It was stained, then spattered with liquids that caused the stain to blur and run in cloudlike formations.

ALBERTINE: An opaque white glass, decorated with enameled floral designs. Also known as Crown Milano.

ALEXANDRITE: Glass containing heat-sensitive chemicals that caused it to shade from pale citron yellow to rose and then bluish purple.

AMBERINA: A transparent glass containing gold, causing it to shade from amber to ruby red when reheated.

AVENTURINE: A yellow or green glass containing fine-grained copper or chrome particles that sparkle.

BURMESE: Contains uranium oxide or gold, which caused it to shade from yellow to pink in areas that were reheated; it was made in glossy and satin finishes.

CAMEO: Made in layers, usually of different colors, and then carved to create raised cameo designs.

CASED GLASS: Made in layers of different colors by blowing linings of additional glass into an outer shell. Cased glass, like Cameo *(above)*, is often cut.

CORAL: Red-to-yellow shading created by covering an opaque body with a layer of heat-sensitive glass.

CORALENE: An applied decoration of glass beads, used on any glass, usually in the form of coral-like branches.

CRAQUELLE: Rough-textured glass made by either plunging molten glass into cold water or rolling it in crushed glass, then quickly reheating, blowing and shaping it.

CROWN MILANO: See Albertine.

CUT GLASS: Glass with designs cut by grinding it.

ENAMELED GLASS: Coated with glossy, heat-fused paint.

ENGRAVED GLASS: Glass decorated with carved designs made with hand tools or an engraving wheel.

ETCHED GLASS: Creating a design by coating with wax, then routing the design into wax in the area to be etched.

FLASHED GLASS: A transparent glass thinly coated inside with glass of another color to give a shaded effect.

FROSTED GLASS: Glass sprayed with acid and potassium fluoride for a dull mat finish.

LATTICINIO: Decoration of swirling, interlocking enameled threads embedded in the glass before it was blown.

LAVA GLASS: Opaque black glass, often with colored inserts, made by adding lava to the molten mixture.

MARY GREGORY GLASS: Translucent colored glass decorated with white figures of children; it was named after a New England artist who specialized in such subjects.

MERCURY GLASS: A double-walled glass with a coating of mercury or silver nitrate applied between the layers.

MILLEFIORI: Literally "thousand flowers," made by joining colored glass rods into flower formations and fusing them into canes before the glass was blown.

MOSS AGATA: Splashed with colored ground glass to resemble natural agate.

MOTHER-OF-PEARL: Glass with indentations in which air was trapped between layers.

NAPOLI: Decorated in enamel and gilt outside and inside.

OPAL GLASS: Opaque white, cream or pale beige glass imitating porcelain. Also known as Milk Glass.

PATTERN-MOLDED GLASS: A glass blown first against a mold, to impress a pattern, then blown full size.

PEACH BLOW: Made with heat-sensitive chemicals to create shades from rose to white, yellow or pale blue.

PEARL SATIN: See Mother-of-Pearl.

PLATED GLASS: A glass made in several layers by dipping blown glass into a second color, forming an overlay.

POMONA: Acid-etched, frosted glass with clear designs.

ROSE AMBER: See Amberina.

ROYAL FLEMISH: Crystal glass, inspired by stained-glass windows, with raised enamel and gilt dividing lines.

SATIN GLASS: Translucent glass, usually colored, with an acid-finished mat surface; often the colored glass was lined with a layer of white milk glass.

SILVERED GLASS: See Mercury Glass.

SPANGLED GLASS: Opaque or transparent glass embedded with metallic flakes, sometimes covered with a thin layer of colored glass to make the flakes sparkle.

SPATTER GLASS: Opaque or clear glass, sometimes colored, with embedded colors. Also called Splashed glass.

STAINED GLASS: Clear glass painted with metallic stain in imitation of colored glasses. The stain is easily scratched.

THREADED GLASS: Glass decorated with thin parallel strands of colored or clear glass.

VASA MURRHINA: Clear-coated glass that has been embedded with metallic flakes and bits of colored glass.

WHEELING PEACH BLOW: See Coral.

WILD ROSE: See Peach Blow.

brought over their expertise in color technology, engraving and cutting, which had made them the masters of the glass industry throughout the world.

The boom in American art glass did not really start until 1883, when Joseph Locke of the New England Glass Company invented and patented a method of shading colored glass by reheating it. Locke's original glass, called Amberina, was shaded amber to ruby red in the reheated areas. It proved to be so popular that one company, the Mt. Washington Glass Co. of New Bedford, Massachusetts, went so far as to imitate Amberina directly. Its version is indistinguishable, even by experts, from that of the New England Glass Co., but—under the prodding of a patent-infringement suit—it changed the name of its glass to Rose Amber.

Beginning collectors may hear the story that Amberina was created accidentally, when a gold ring slipped off a glassworker's finger into a pot of molten glass. The story is apocryphal, but there is a grain of truth in the tale: a small amount of gold does go into the making of Amberina. It is the gold that causes the change of color from amber to ruby. However, the gold must be powdered when it is added to the other ingredients. A gold ring would simply sink to the bottom of the pot.

Encouraged by the success of Amberina, other heat-sensitive glasses were created in short order—shading from yellow to pink, from red to pale yellow, from rose to yellow and then blue. Glassmakers introduced metallic flakes, colored glass beads, and colored glass threads and rods into molten glass; they also applied beads and rods to the surface. They etched the glass and dipped it in acid baths to create frosted, crackled and satin-finish effects; and they made glass look like opal, onyx, agate, lava, mother-of-pearl and tortoise shell. They painted it, cut it, engraved it and layered it, removing some of the layers afterward to disclose the different colored glass beneath. (For a description of each of these forms of art glass, see the listing at left.)

In this inventive atmosphere, American art glass quickly surpassed its European forebears. While decorative glassware continued to be made in Europe—and is a part of many collections, including my own—the most varied and ingenious designs were produced in the United States. Indeed, some ware was made abroad under license from American manufacturers—the most notable being the small vase *(page 62)* made of Burmese glass, a heat-treated type with yellow-to-pink shading, which became very popular in Britain after Queen Victoria ordered a tea set made of it. As a result, most collectors concentrate on the American products.

Some kinds, naturally, are easier to find and more easily affordable than others. A modest collection can be built around Amberina, for instance, which was made by many companies in many forms—bowls, plates, finger bowls, tumblers, toothpick holders. However, for varieties—such as an Amberina cookie jar, a form seldom made—the price rises.

Selecting art glass is partly a matter of taste. Some people emphasize color or shape alone. There are Amberina collectors, for example, who concentrate on hunting for pieces in which the normal shading, from red at the top to amber at the base, is reversed. Others specialize in examples of Amberina in which the reddish shade at the top is fuchsia rather than ruby.

But the condition of the piece is also an important factor. Examine it carefully for cracks or chips, or for breaks that may have been mended and disguised by polishing. Is it a piece that is complete in itself, or should it have a lid or be part of a set? This is not to say that a cracked jar or one without a lid should be avoided. If a flawed piece was originally produced in limited numbers, perhaps for some commemorative purpose, it may still be of value. So may a piece that is rarely if ever found in perfect condition. Very few art-glass baskets, for instance, have survived intact; their handles almost always have been broken.

Breakage, in fact, is the major problem in owning art glass. Ideally, it should be kept on open display, preferably on the window sill, where it will catch the light. And I do not hesitate to use less valuable pieces for the purposes for which they were intended—I put flowers in my flower vases and candy in my candy jars. But I have adopted certain procedures for minimizing damage when pieces must be handled. I avoid sudden temperature changes, sometimes to the extent of wearing gloves when I must pick up glass from a cold window sill. If the glass needs washing, I use a plastic dishpan and wash each piece separately in lukewarm water and mild detergent. I also rinse each piece separately in a second plastic pan of lukewarm water, never under the faucet. Finally, I air-dry it. With these few precautions a collection of art glass can be enjoyed in everyday use.

The best stocks of art glass will be found in antique shops specializing in Victoriana, but much is also sold at general antique shows. Antiques magazines frequently advertise pieces for sale. Best of all, the lucky and perceptive collector may be able to spot unrecognized art glass at thrift shops and flea markets. Such bargain hunting is perhaps the most exciting form of collecting, and it is simplified in the case of art glass because detailed descriptions of valuable pieces can be found in the large number of books, some of which are listed on page 69, that have been written about the major factories and their products.

For related material, see the articles on Bottles, Carnival Glass, Depression Glass, Jars, Lalique, Pressed Glass and Tiffany Glass in separate volumes of this encyclopedia.

58 / ART GLASS

Peach Blow, a shaded glass, was made by several companies. The examples here are an apple-shaped sugar bowl and a decorative pear from Hobbs, Brockunier & Company and two paperweights, an apple and a peach, from the New England Glass Company.

ART GLASS / 59

A melon-shaped vase of Napoli glass displays its typical see-through design—gold lines outside and colored flower shapes inside.

A Napoli glass bowl, decorated on both surfaces, rests on a 10-inch metal stand, whose free-flowing curves anticipate Art Nouveau.

The rough texture of this covered melon-shaped bowl and leaf-shaped saucer identifies them as Craquelle. The bowl is 6 inches high.

A 7½-inch jar of Royal Flemish, a stained glass with raised, gilded lines, may have been intended as a container for biscuits or crackers.

60 / ART GLASS

Satin glass, with its soft mat finish, was often a vehicle for other decorative effects. The spiraling design of the tall vase is created by pulling and twisting molten glass. The small vase with a pleated mouth (left) is set in a Japanese-style mounting known as Mat-Su-No-ke. The diamond-patterned bowl in Pearl Satin glass (right) is embellished with spangles and applied ornaments.

The mottling that decorates these two vases is characteristic of Agata glass. The effect was achieved with a combination of stain and mineral spirits that was commonly applied to a shaded translucent glass called Peach Blow. Usually Agata glass was shiny, like the 7-inch lily vase, so called because of its shape. In the rarer mat green vase at left, the Agata effect is used only as rim decoration.

62 / ART GLASS

Burmese glass, with its pale yellow to pink shading, was an American invention that also became popular in Britain. The British Burmese vase with a ruffled rim (left) and the American Burmese urn have both been acid-etched to produce a soft, velvety finish.

ART GLASS / 63

Painted flowers in enamel and gilt decorate the surface of two shaded Burmese glass vases. The richly ornamented 10-inch vase on the left has in addition an allover scalloped design between the two layers of glass, and a mother-of-pearl finish.

64 / ART GLASS

Two ancient Italian processes adapted by Victorian art-glass manufacturers were the filigree caning technique known as Latticinio, seen on the striped bottle, juice glass and vase, and Millefiori, the floral technique that decorates the French-made vase at right.

This Pattern-molded bowl of amber glass was first blown into a mold to impress the diamond-quilted pattern on the inside. Then threads of clear glass were wound around the outside, and a clear edging was applied.

Opal glass served as the base for these five pieces of art glass. At the top, left to right, are a painted vase that imitates Dresden china, an apricot-tinted vase and a gilt-trimmed tumbler. At the bottom are flower bowls, one decorated with acorns (left), the other with daisies.

66 / ART GLASS

A Cameo-glass ewer, its design created by cutting through the outer of two layers of glass, is fitted with a metal top. The piece was made in England by Thomas Webb & Sons, a firm that served the U.S. market.

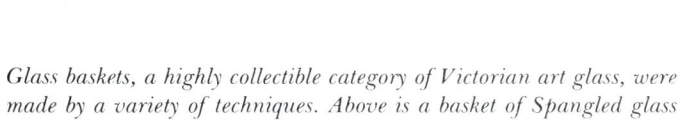

ART GLASS / 67

Glass baskets, a highly collectible category of Victorian art glass, were made by a variety of techniques. Above is a basket of Spangled glass flecked with characteristic metallic flakes; at right is a basket of Pearl Satin glass in a typical diamond-quilted pattern.

The contrasting colors of a ribbed and fluted bowl, 12 inches in diameter and ornamented with gold flowers, identify it as Cased glass, formed by combining partially blown glass with additional layers of glass before blowing the piece into its final shape.

A DIRECTORY OF ART-GLASS MANUFACTURERS

Only a handful of American glassware manufacturers were involved to any extent in the production of Victorian art glass, and most of them identified their wares in one form or another, making it relatively easy for collectors to authenticate an unfamiliar piece. Some manufacturers imprinted what is known as a factory mark on the bottom of their products, in the form of the company's name or initials. The New England Glass Company, for instance, marked its wares N.E.G. Co.

Other manufacturers identified their art glass with the name of the man who designed it, a so-called designer's mark. Although this is a clue to the period of the piece, it is not necessarily a guide to the manufacturer because designers occasionally shifted their allegiance from company to company.

A third clue to the origin of art glass is the type mark. Many manufacturers identified their wares with the names given to various kinds of glass—Burmese or Cameo, for instance—although sometimes the type mark is given simply as an initial. Crown Milano, for example, is frequently marked with a CM or with a single C or M.

The directory at right lists the major art-glass manufacturers, along with the names of the most important men who designed for them and the names of the types of glass with which each company is associated. But a piece of art glass that contains none of this information is not necessarily a fake. Unfortunately, manufacturers sometimes placed this information on a paper label that was peeled off or fell off with the passage of time.

BOSTON & SANDWICH GLASS COMPANY
Sandwich, Massachusetts

Founded in 1825 by Deming Jarves; ceased production in 1888. Produced Craquelle, Mary Gregory, Satin, Silvered, Threaded, Latticinio, Opal.

BOSTON SILVER GLASS COMPANY
Cambridge, Massachusetts

Established in 1857; in operation until 1871. Produced Silvered glass.

CAPE COD GLASS WORKS
Sandwich, Massachusetts

Established in 1858, also by Deming Jarves, and operated in close association with Boston & Sandwich Glass Company *(above)* until 1882. Produced Cut glass, Pressed glass, Vasa Murrhina.

HOBBS, BROCKUNIER & COMPANY
Wheeling, West Virginia

Founded in 1820 as the Virginia Green Glassworks; name changed to Hobbs, Brockunier & Company in 1863; was nation's largest until 1891 merger that formed United States Glass. Produced Wheeling Peach Blow and Spangled glass, both created by William Leighton. Also produced Pressed Amberina and Craquelle.

LIBBEY GLASS COMPANY
Toledo, Ohio

Established in 1888 by William L. Libbey; produced Amberina and Pomona.

MT. WASHINGTON GLASS WORKS
New Bedford, Massachusetts

Established in 1837 in Boston, moved to New Bedford in 1869; merged with Pairpoint Manufacturing Co., a silver-plating firm, in 1894. Head designers were two brothers, Alfred and Harry Smith, who set up a successful decorating department in 1871. Albert Stefflin designed the firm's Queen's Burmese ware. Mt. Washington produced Albertine, Burmese, Cameo, Crown Milano, Cut glass, Engraved glass, Lava, Mary Gregory, Napoli, Opal, Peach Blow, Pearl Satin, Rose Amber, Royal Flemish and Silvered glass.

NEW ENGLAND GLASS COMPANY
East Cambridge, Massachusetts

Established in 1814 as Boston Porcelain & Glass Manufacturing Co.; name changed to New England Glass Co. in 1818; in operation until 1888. Produced Amberina, Agata and Silvered glass, designed by Joseph Locke. The company's other products were Cameo, Pomona and Wild Rose.

PHOENIX GLASS COMPANY
Pittsburgh, Pennsylvania

Established in 1880; produced Mother-of-Pearl, designed by Joseph Webb.

SMITH BROTHERS
New Bedford, Massachusetts

Established in 1876; ceased operation around 1893. Produced Cut and Engraved glass, Enameled and Gilded glass and Pattern-molded glass.

UNION GLASS COMPANY
Somerville, Massachusetts

Established in 1854; in operation until 1924. Produced Cut and Engraved glass, Silvered glass.

MUSEUMS

The Art Institute of Chicago
Chicago, Illinois 60603

Bennington Museum
Bennington, Vermont 05201

John Nelson Bergstrom Art Center and Museum
Neenah, Wisconsin 54956

Carnegie Institute Museum of Art
Pittsburgh, Pennsylvania 15213

Chrysler Museum at Norfolk
Norfolk, Virginia 23510

The Corning Museum of Glass and Glass Center
Corning, New York 14830

The Currier Gallery of Art
Manchester, New Hampshire 03104

Henry Ford Museum
Dearborn, Michigan 48121

Marathon County Historical Society
Wausau, Wisconsin 54401

The New-York Historical Society
New York, New York 10024

New Bedford Glass Museum
New Bedford, Massachusetts 12742

Newcomb College
Tulane University
New Orleans, Louisiana 70118

Old Sturbridge Village
Sturbridge, Massachusetts 01566

Oglebay Institute-Mansion Museum
Wheeling, West Virginia 26003

Sandwich Glass Museum
Sandwich, Massachusetts 02563

Smithsonian Institution
Museum of History and Technology
Washington, D.C. 20560

Toledo Museum of Art
Toledo, Ohio 43697

Wadsworth Atheneum
Hartford, Connecticut 06103

COLLECTORS ORGANIZATIONS

Glass Collectors' Club of Toledo
P.O. Box 2695
Toledo, Ohio 43606

BOOKS

Avila, George C., *The Pairpoint Glass Story.* Reynolds-DeWalt Printing, Inc., 1968.

Barrett, Richard Carter, *A Collector's Handbook of Blown and Pressed American Glass.* Forward's Color Production, Inc., 1971.

Bridgeman, Harriet, and Elizabeth Drury, *The Encyclopedia of Victoriana.* Macmillan Publishing Co., Inc., 1975.

Butler, Joseph T., *American Antiques 1800-1900.* Odyssey Press, 1965.

Darr, Patrick, *A Guide to Art and Pattern Glass.* Pilgrim House Publishing Co., 1960.

Grover, Ray and Lee:
Art Glass Nouveau. Charles E. Tuttle Co., Inc., 1967.
Contemporary Art Glass. Crown Publishers, Inc., 1975.
Carved and Decorated European Glass. Charles E. Tuttle Co., Inc., 1970.

Innes, Lowell, *Pittsburgh Glass 1797-1891: A History and Guide for Collectors.* Houghton Mifflin Company, 1976.

Lee, Ruth Webb:
Nineteenth Century Art Glass. M. Barrows & Company, Inc., 1952.
Victorian Glass. Lee Publications, 1944.
Sandwich Glass. Lee Publications, revised 1947.

McClinton, Katharine M., *Collecting American Victorian Antiques.* Charles Scribner's Sons, 1966.

McKearin, George S. and Helen:
American Glass. Crown Publishers, Inc., revised 1948.
Two Hundred Years of American Blown Glass. Doubleday & Company, Inc., revised 1966.

Papert, Emma, *The Illustrated Guide to American Glass.* Hawthorn Books, Inc., 1972.

Revi, Albert C., *Nineteenth-Century Glass, Its Genesis and Development.* Thomas Nelson & Sons, 1959.

Schwartz, Marvin D., *Collector's Guide to Antique American Glass.* Doubleday & Company, Inc., 1969.

Toledo Museum of Art, The:
Libbey Glass, A Tradition of 150 Years. Toledo Museum of Art, 1968.
New England Glass Co. 1818-1888. Toledo Museum of Art, 1963.

Wilson, Kenneth M., *New England Glass and Glassmaking.* Old Sturbridge, Inc., 1972.

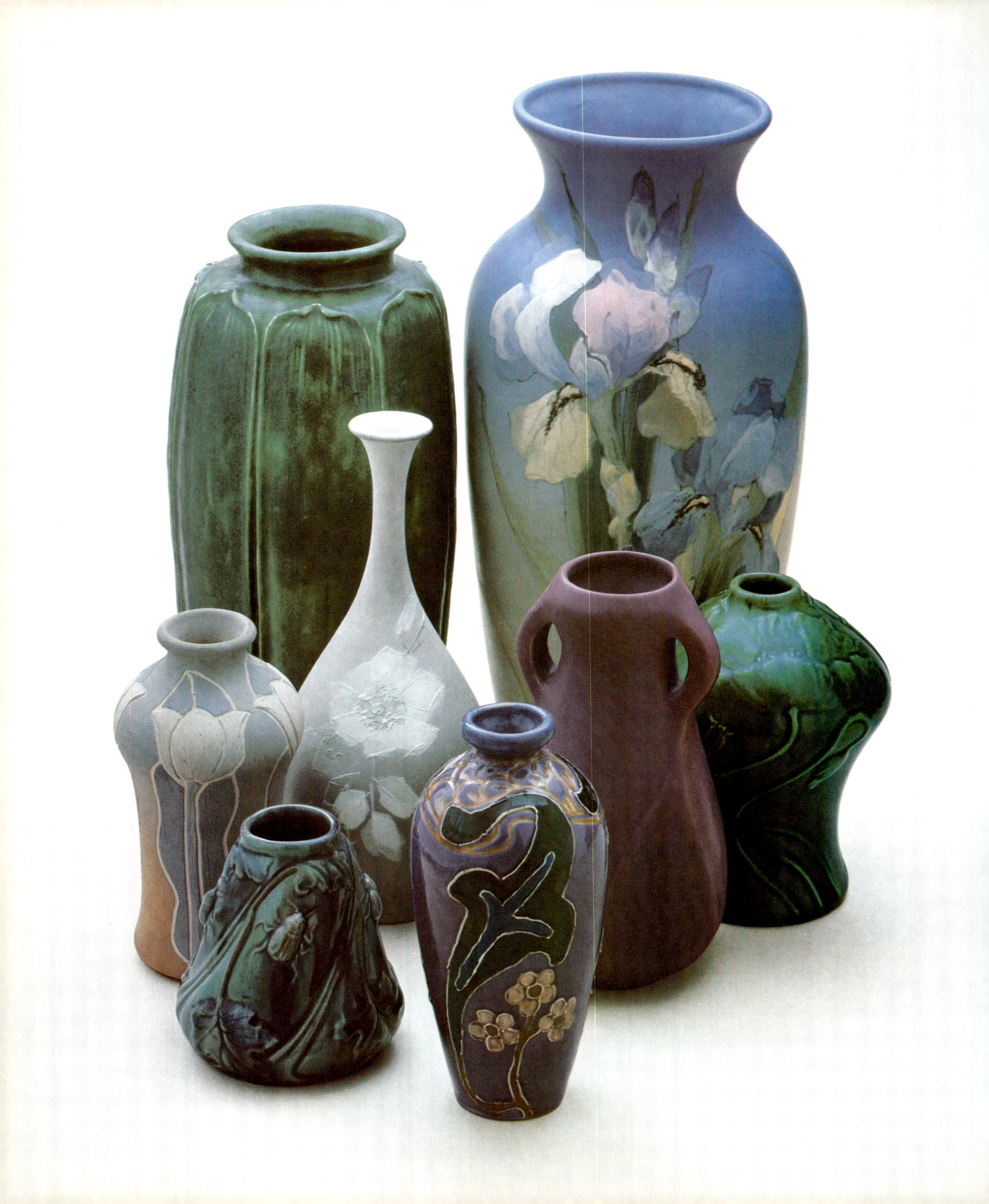

Art Pottery
Artifacts With Social Significance

Art pottery, simply defined, is any ceramic vessel created for beauty rather than utility, even though it may incidentally serve a practical purpose as a vase, pitcher, fruit or candy dish, or even dinner plate. But as used by collectors, the term refers to American ceramics made over a specific period—half a century ending just after World War I—and to a specific artistic philosophy, one that placed great emphasis on idiosyncratic handcraftsmanship. The products of this unique time are valued for their esthetic qualities. But they have a special interest to collectors because of their history.

The art pottery movement—and it was indeed a movement—involved a galaxy of fascinating people,

Rosalie M. Berberian, a public-health teacher and researcher, has been collecting art pottery since 1970.

many of them women and a few wildly eccentric, responding to several different social forces that became important during the latter part of the 19th Century. One of these forces was an intellectual rebellion against the machine-made anonymity of the mass-produced products of the Industrial Revolution. It began in England, where the artist William Morris, seeking to revive the good old days of the individual artisan, established whole groups of cottage industries devoted to handmade textiles, glass, pottery and furniture, and it quickly took root in America.

The handicrafts idea had a special appeal to well-to-do American women, who played a leading role in the

Among the many decorative techniques employed by American art potters, eight of the more popular are illustrated by the vases at left. The green vase at the top was decorated with leaf forms pressed onto the wet clay; on the blue vase the irises were painted on with colored slip, or liquid clay. In the center row, the tulip design on the vase at left was incised in the clay, while the rose on the vase next to it was a freehand addition. The smooth mat glaze of the handled vase was sprayed on with an atomizer. Next to it, the poppy design was probably made by pressing a slab of wet clay over a mold before shaping it, while the cone-shaped vase at the bottom was probably cast in a mold. On the glossy vase at the bottom, the free-form leaf was outlined with slip squeezed through a nozzle. The vases range in height from 4½ to 15 inches.

creation of art pottery. Some were seeking useful outlets for their creative talents; others sought to help women find a place in industry and the arts. They founded pottery businesses, taught ceramic design and became craftworkers of memorable skill.

Intricately intertwined with the efforts of these gifted, wealthy and high-minded amateurs were those of hardheaded, perceptive businessmen. They sensed a new sophistication in American taste and were quick to begin turning out lines of hand-crafted art pottery along with the commercial products they had already been making.

The generally accepted birthdate for the art pottery movement is 1876, the year of the Centennial Exposition in Philadelphia. At that fair, American potters were exposed to magnificent displays of European and Oriental ceramics. Potters from Ohio, which had long been a center of the ceramics industry, were particularly impressed with what they saw.

Back home in Cincinnati, working in various small shops—among them the Coultry Pottery, the Dallas Pottery, and T. J. Wheatley and Company—they discovered the secret of French barbotine ware, with its decorations in low relief and colorful underglaze. It involved the use of slip, or watered-down clay, into which chemicals were introduced that changed color on firing. Using this technique, they experimented and produced wares that became known as Cincinnati Limoges, after the city in France where most barbotine was made.

Thus began an investigation of techniques that carried American potters far beyond the European and Oriental models that had inspired them. Glazes, firing temperatures, modes of inscribing or applying decoration, the behavior and composition of clay—the American potters experimented with them all. They used the heavy, coarse clay of earthenware and the fine, strong clay of porcelain with glaze coatings of many kinds—mat-surfaced and shiny, opaque and translucent, some that turned crystalline in the fire and others that crackled or swirled. They laid on their decorations with brushes, squeezed them on through tubes, sprayed them on with atomizers. They shaped the wet clay with their hands and with molds, carved its surface in high, low and reverse relief, and hammered it like metal.

Before the art pottery movement had run its course it

resulted in the establishment of well over a hundred producers in 23 states from coast to coast. A large number clustered, understandably, around the rich clay deposits of Ohio, and several appeared in the arts-and-crafts colonies of Colorado and California. But some of the most notable sprang up in such unlikely places as Louisiana, Mississippi and the industrial suburbs of Boston. Many of them were studio potteries, owned and run by individual potters working with a few assistants after the cottage-industry example of William Morris. Others were studios operated by commercial firms as a prestigious sideline to dinnerware and chimney flues.

One of the first and perhaps the most important of the major art potteries was the Rookwood Pottery, established in Cincinnati in 1880 by a wealthy woman—Maria Longworth Nichols Storer, whose family were great patrons of the arts. Her work force was largely female, women of means who, like herself, had come to pottery by dabbling in the ladylike hobby of china painting—decorating plain china plates with hand-painted designs. After Rookwood became a commercial success it was no longer run by amateurs: Mrs. Storer installed a manager, and things, in her words, "began to assume a business air." The early output of Rookwood, dating from about 1880 to 1884, has been rather politely described as wildly experimental. Mrs. Storer and her potters went in heavily for gilding, carving and incising.

Gradually, however, the Rookwood style became more controlled and the potters turned their attention almost exclusively to applying decorations with under-

Two examples of the pottery known as Cincinnati Limoges—a vase encrusted with sea shells and seaweed, 14¾ inches tall, and a flower-trimmed platter, 11 inches wide—stand beside a French barbotine vase they imitate. In attempting to duplicate the designs of imported ceramics, first seen in the U.S. at the 1876 Centennial Exposition, American potters developed their own styles and techniques.

glaze, the technique borrowed from French barbotine. Beginning in 1884, the Rookwood potters sprayed on the underglaze slip with an atomizer, to achieve even more subtly shaded effects and, from 1884 to 1898, they added increasingly sophisticated underglaze paintings of such subjects as flowers, birds, seascapes and landscapes. A typical bottle-shaped vase *(below)* has a raised, three-dimensional sculpture of a crab against an underglaze painting of seaweed backed, in turn, by a shaded mustard-yellow background.

This Rookwood technique was soon copied by neighboring potteries and it became the hallmark of all Ohio pottery produced around the turn of the century. From Rookwood itself came the famed Standard, or brown-glazed, ware, which has blurred background colors of brown, yellow and green topped by a hard, clear, pale-yellow glaze *(bottom right)*. A number of other Ohio potteries, notably those around Zanesville, developed their own versions of Rookwood Standard. Chief among them were the big three commercial potteries—Weller, Owens and Roseville—but the imitators also included

A sculpted ceramic crab was applied to the surface of an 1885 vase decorated with an underwater scene of swirling seaweed. It was made by the Rookwood Pottery, an early and influential Ohio art pottery.

A Rookwood vase 6½ inches tall, highly glazed but softly colored, stands in front of an imitation from the Weller Pottery. Rookwood called this style Standard; Weller called its version Louwelsa.

74 / ART POTTERY

A crackle-glazed plate from the Dedham Pottery displays a border of hand-painted rabbits, one of the pottery's more popular designs.

the smaller Zanesville Art Pottery, the Cambridge Art Pottery in Cambridge, Ohio, and the Lonhuda Pottery in Steubenville. On the other side of the country, the Stockton Art Pottery in Stockton, California, also produced a brown-glazed ware similar to Rookwood Standard. Each gave its ware a special name: Weller's was called Louwelsa; Owens', Utopian; Roseville's, Rozane Royal Dark; Stockton's, Rekston; Cambridge's, Terrhea; Zanesville's, La Moro. By the 1970s examples of these wares were bringing thousands of dollars at sales.

Around the same time that Rookwood was experimenting with underglaze decoration, Hugh C. Robertson, a member of an illustrious family of Massachusetts art potters, was exploring the same technique. Working at first at the family's Chelsea Keramic Art Works and later at a factory in Dedham, Robertson created the barbotine-inspired Bourg-la-Reine of Chelsea, decorated with underglaze slip mostly in tones of blue and green, as well as terra-cotta imitations of ancient Greek vases. Other products made by the Robertson firm included pottery that was decorated by various techniques while the clay was still wet. Sometimes the moist clay was incised, sometimes sculpted and sometimes impressed with materials like grasses and flowers to

Identical vases with square handles and dolphin feet show the different styles of artists of the Chelsea Keramic Art Works. Josephine Day initialed the vase bearing the sculpted ceramic roses. The painted vase was the work of Hugh C. Robertson, whose family owned the works.

Two decorative tiles from the Grueby-Faience Company bear the flat mat-glaze finish that the Grueby Pottery later applied to its vases and bowls. Grueby's nonshiny finish started a trend that spread through the art pottery movement after the turn of the century.

create designs in reverse relief. In one technique, the moist clay was hammered in the manner of metalsmiths to produce a dimpled metal-like surface.

Robertson also tried to capture the rich and flowing glazes of Oriental pottery. His deep oxblood-red glaze is characteristic of Chinese pottery of the 17th Century K'ang Hsi period. In addition he developed a number of other brilliant glazes—sea green, apple green, mustard yellow, turquoise blue—most of which he applied in the style of Oriental potters, using the glazes to create crackled finishes as well as flambé, pitted and pockmarked effects. But white crackle-glazed tableware, trimmed with hand-painted blue borders in more than 50 patterns of flora and fauna *(opposite, top)*, eventually became the mainstay of Robertson's commercial output, and the company continued to produce this ware until it closed in 1943.

In sharp contrast to the business-like Robertson was the most imaginative—and most eccentric—of the early art potters, George E. Ohr, who operated a one-man pottery in Biloxi, Mississippi, beginning around 1883. Ohr dug his own clay from the banks of the Mississippi, transported it upstream on a barge and loaded it on a horse-drawn wagon to carry it to his Biloxi Art Pottery. He threw his pots on a wheel, shaping each slightly differently because, he said, God never made two things alike. He formulated his own glazes and fired his ware in a hand-built kiln.

Ohr's work is characterized by eggshell-thin walls, and though some of his shapes are conventional, most of his work was squeezed, folded, twisted, collapsed, crushed, pinched, pleated and otherwise tortured into bizarre, sometimes grotesque, shapes *(page 77)*. A number of pieces were inscribed with verses, quotations, or the names and addresses of visitors who happened by the pottery. His glazes combined odd, unexpected colors and he produced a mottled glaze now referred to as tortoise-shell. Known at the time as the "Mad Potter" of Biloxi, Ohr is now regarded as an American genius.

One of Ohr's contemporaries—equally inventive but less eccentric—may be said to have signaled the close of the first period of art pottery. Working in his Middle Lane Pottery in East Hampton, New York, Theophilus A. Brouwer developed an unconventional method of handling glazes: he subjected them directly to the flames within the kiln. Brouwer called his technique fire painting, and the result was a free-form pattern of amorphous shapes resembling clouds or sea grasses.

The man generally credited with initiating the change in art pottery design that ushered in the next era is William E. Grueby of Revere, Massachusetts, who rediscovered and exploited the neglected art of mat glazing. Grueby is known for his decorative architectural tiles *(above)*, but he also made the jars and vases that were the staples of most art potters.

Many of Grueby's jars and vases were decorated with thin slabs of clay that were pushed, pulled, curved and rolled into leaf forms that followed the line of the vessel;

76 / ART POTTERY

A misty moon shining through moss-draped trees was the most popular scenic motif for the mat-glazed ware of the Newcomb Pottery in

Louisiana; this 11-inch vase was done after 1910. The high-glazed Newcomb vase incised with a lily design dates from the early 1900s.

in spirit they resembled Art Nouveau but they were not as fluid. The decorations were done freehand by women recruited from art schools in the area: the Boston Museum of Fine Arts School, the Cowels Art School and the Massachusetts Normal School. Though Grueby's wares were an artistic success, the company had financial problems and ceased operation in 1909, leaving the field to an army of imitators all over the country.

One was Newcomb Pottery in New Orleans, which came into being just as advanced education was being opened to women. An outgrowth of the art and design department of Newcomb College, the women's college of Tulane University, Newcomb Pottery was organized in 1895 with the help of Mary G. Sheerer, one of the women who had helped to start Rookwood in Cincinnati. It was intended initially to serve as a laboratory for students, but like Rookwood, it quickly evolved into a successful self-contained business staffed by women.

At first the Newcomb potters followed current fashion and painted or sprayed underglaze designs of native flowers in a flat, two-dimensional style; the designs were then covered with a shiny, transparent glaze. Later the designs were incised into clay while it was wet and the outlines were filled in after an initial firing had firmed it. Then, after 1910, Newcomb picked up the mat glazes employed so successfully by Grueby. The color used most often was a soft, misty blue *(above, left)*, although Newcomb ware also appears in green, mauve and violet.

While small potteries like Newcomb concentrated on a single style, based usually on one technique, the large potteries like Rookwood, Owens, Weller and Roseville were turning out quantities of artware in a multiplicity of styles—to satisfy what had become, by the turn of the century, an insatiable market. Their work was heavily influenced by one man, Frederick H. Rhead, whose wares are much sought after by collectors and are likely

Both the eccentricity and the remarkable skill of George Ohr, the "Mad Potter" of Biloxi, Mississippi, are demonstrated by these three vases, ranging from 4½ to 8 inches high. All three have walls of exceptional thinness and Ohr's typical running and mottled glazes.

In his pottery in East Hampton, New York, Theophilus Brouwer created an eggshell-thin vase with ceramic leaves and finished it with his famed "fire-painting" glaze by exposing the pot to the flame.

to be priced rather high. Rhead came to the United States in 1902 from England, where he had been art director of a Staffordshire pottery works before the age of 20. Between 1902 and 1908 he worked for three potteries in Ohio—Roseville, Weller and Vance/Avon Faience. Then he went to the Jervis Pottery in Oyster Bay, New York, and from there drifted westward, leaving his mark on art potteries across the country until, in 1913, he settled in southern California and established the Rhead Pottery near Santa Barbara.

Rhead had no skill at throwing pots and admitted it, but he was a remarkable designer. He developed many formulas for glazes, and a technique of outlining his designs with trails of thin white slip. The technique is now known as squeeze-bag *(page 78)* because the slip was squeezed from a cloth bag fitted with a nozzle, in much the way cooks squeeze icing from pastry bags onto cakes. Rhead's best-known works are Della Robbia and an Aztec pattern, which was done for Roseville, and a Japanese-inspired line called Jap Birdimal, designed for Weller. One of my own objectives as a collector is to have examples of Rhead's output for each of the potteries he was associated with.

Despite the names Rhead gave his pottery—Jap Birdi-

78 / ART POTTERY

A vase from the short-lived Craven Art Pottery (1904-1908) shows a drawing made by Frederick Rhead's "squeeze bag" technique.

A three-handled vase glazed one color inside, and unglazed outside, shows how Art Nouveau influenced the pottery of Louis C. Tiffany.

mal, Aztec, Della Robbia—his work was clearly derived from French Art Nouveau. But the most prominent exponent of this style was a contemporary of Rhead's: Artus Van Briggle. Van Briggle came to the Rookwood Pottery in the 1890s and showed such promise as a designer that the pottery sent him abroad to study. In Europe he was completely captivated by Art Nouveau.

On his return to America Van Briggle worked briefly for Rookwood, until tuberculosis forced him to move west to a drier climate. In 1901 he established his own pottery in Colorado Springs, and began to fashion vessels whose walls incorporated conventionalized floral and animal motifs, and sometimes even human forms, done in flowing, melting lines. In many cases, the whole vase or bowl was like a single piece of sculpture, although in fact Van Briggle achieved his effects by casting his designs in molds.

In 1904, just a few years after he moved west, Van Briggle died. But his widow took over his pottery, which flourished and grew, continuing into the 1970s to produce vases from some of the earliest and most famous of Van Briggle's molds. As a result, examples are not difficult to find. The earlier pieces, however, are considered more valuable because they are more finely crafted. The molds were not used as many times and the impressions are sharper. In addition, Van Briggle's original glazes produced a particularly beautiful mat finish, so flat that it is spoken of as dry.

Admirers of Art Nouveau who collect Van Briggle and Rhead also prize the work of another artist inspired by this style, Louis Comfort Tiffany. Best known for his glass (see *Tiffany Glass* in a separate volume), Tiffany began producing Art Nouveau pottery in his studio in Corona, New York, in 1905, the year after Van Briggle died. Like Van Briggle, he treated the entire vase or bowl as a piece of sculpture *(above)*. But to achieve his conventionalized designs of flowers and foliage he sometimes sprayed the actual plant material with shellac, then used the stiffened material to cast a plaster

Created in 1901 and still in production three quarters of a century later, a vase by Artus Van Briggle, called Lady of the Lily, is typical of his free-flowing sculptural style. This piece, 10½ inches tall, is glazed in Mountain Craig Brown, a color introduced in the 1920s.

80 / ART POTTERY

The glaze of this Owens Pottery vase glows in many colors when seen under light.

In 1902 the Weller Pottery brought Jacques Sicard from France to design a special collection of art pottery. The result, Sicardo, used iridescent glazes in a palette of hothouse colors like those in the visionary paintings of the French symbolists.

Two vases illustrate the influence of Adelaide Robineau on the art pottery movement. The porcelain vase at left with the luminous glaze was made in her pottery in Syracuse, New York. The white vase was done at the University City Pottery in Missouri, where she taught.

For years art potters used conventionalized designs, as on this tree-decorated vase from a pottery in Marblehead, Massachusetts.

This flowered bowl bears the mark of the Saturday Evening Girls program for young immigrant women at Boston's Revere Pottery.

mold. Tiffany's first art pottery was relatively restrained. It was glazed in a light yellow shading into a darker tone, which is often called Old Ivory. Around 1906, he began using a variety of glazes—mat, iridescent, crystalline—and then in 1911 he introduced the most dramatic glaze of all, Bronze Pottery, which was glazed with a thin coating of the metal itself.

Tiffany art pottery is scarce and relatively expensive, partly because the Tiffany studio produced very little of it after 1914. But it is also difficult to find because Tiffany withdrew his pieces from stores if they had not been sold after three months, and either gave them away or destroyed them.

In its final flowering, the art pottery movement adopted a modified, Americanized version of the Art Nouveau style—more severe than the original—and experimented with new clays and new glazes. Three of the more interesting potteries of this period were directly or indirectly outgrowths of the women's movement.

Like the women who formed the nucleus of the early Rookwood Pottery, Adelaide Alsop Robineau was a well-to-do amateur whose hobby was china painting. But she soon became bored with decorating ready-made china forms, and with the encouragement of her husband started the Robineau Pottery in Syracuse, New York. Mrs. Robineau was fascinated with porcelain and fortunately could afford to be. Porcelain requires a special clay, called kaolin, and a kiln that fires at much higher temperatures than those required for ordinary pottery. Many Robineau porcelains were intricately carved on bodies of almost eggshell thinness, and they were finished in soft mat glazes in an unusual palette of colors—coppery reds and greens, creamy white, deep blue, flame reds, purple-brown.

In 1909, Robineau was invited to join the faculty of a pottery associated with People's University in University City, Missouri, on the outskirts of St. Louis, and for 18 months was associated with one of the more curious educational experiments of American history. People's University was launched by Edward G. Lewis, a St. Louis businessman who was interested in the women's movement, partly out of philanthropy, partly for profit.

People's University was set up primarily as a correspondence school for women. But students who showed exceptional promise were invited to attend classes at the campus in University City. There courses were offered in business, language, journalism, photography and ceramics—and the faculty for the latter was distinguished

POTTERY-MAKING TERMS

BARBOTINE: French pottery decorated with a glaze of liquid clay, or "slip"

BISQUE: Pottery fired at low heat to harden clay

CRACKLEWARE: Pottery covered with a glaze designed to form a network of fine lines when fired

CRAZING: Formation of hairline cracks in a glaze

CRYSTALLINE GLAZE: A glaze designed to form crystals as it cools

ENAMEL GLAZE: A richly colored, opaque glaze

FAIENCE: Pottery made of coarse-grained clay called earthenware, decorated with bright, opaque glazes

FIRING: The process of hardening clay or melting glazes by heating ceramic vessels in a kiln

FLAMBÉ: Glazes giving streaked, flamelike patterns

GILDING: Decoration of gold or other yellow metal

GLAZE: A coating, applied to ceramic ware, that melts when fired, then hardens, making the clay nonporous

GREENWARE: Air-dried pottery that is not yet fired

HIGH-FIRED GLAZE: Glaze fired above 1,190°C. for unusual effects of coloring or design

HIGH GLAZE: A glaze with a smooth, shiny surface

IRIDESCENT GLAZE: Glaze colors that change in different light

KILN: An oven for firing pottery

LUSTER GLAZE: A thin metallic film, often gold, silver or copper, coating a decorated ceramic vessel

MAT GLAZE: An opaque glaze with little or no sheen

OVERGLAZE: Decoration over a glazed background

PORCELAIN: Translucent ceramic made of exceptionally fine-grained clay fired at very high temperatures

SGRAFFITO: Lines scratched through a layer of slip, or liquid clay, before glazing to reveal the clay body

SLIP: A mixture of clay and water, usually about the consistency of heavy cream, that is painted on clay vessels to smooth or decorate the surface before firing

THROWING: The process of forming pottery by hand from a clay ball centered on a spinning potter's wheel

UNDERGLAZE: Decoration applied to unfired ware and glazed, often to create a bas-relief effect

VOLCANIC WARE: Pottery characterized by a bubbly, pock-marked surface, like lava

Dickens' Ware, made by Weller Pottery, was decorated with outline drawings scratched into the damp clay before glazing.

indeed. In addition to Robineau it included Frederick Rhead and the famous French ceramist Taxile Doat, from the staff of the National Manufactory of Sèvres. Doat was a specialist in porcelain design.

The ceramics produced under this faculty were widely exhibited and received many prizes. They were noted for the fineness of their clay bodies and for their glazes, which included, along with the popular mat green, a luminous mat white, an Oriental crackle glaze and a textured glaze called alligator skin. But People's University was disbanded in 1911 when founder Lewis was prosecuted for mail fraud. He moved to California, where he founded the American Woman's Republic and for a time toyed with the idea of reestablishing his

ART POTTERY MARKS

Almost every art pottery marked its wares with a name, monogram or symbol like those below. Some marks aid in dating the pottery: of Robineau's five marks, the letters A-R identify early, experimental work. Rookwood added a flame point to its mark each year, beginning in 1886, until the flames made a circle; thereafter it added a Roman numeral (below is 1901).

| CHELSEA KERAMIC ART WORKS | DEDHAM | GRUEBY | MARBLEHEAD |

| BROUWER, MIDDLE LANE | NEWCOMB COLLEGE | SATURDAY EVENING GIRLS, PAUL REVERE |

ROBINEAU

| ROOKWOOD | LOUIS COMFORT TIFFANY | UNIVERSITY CITY |

| VAN BRIGGLE | VOLKMAR POTTERY | T.J. WHEATLEY |

A DIRECTORY OF ART POTTERIES

Between 1870 and 1920, there were 118 art potteries operating in 23 states, listed below alphabetically in a compilation prepared by pottery expert Paul Evans. Some of the potteries stayed in business continuously; others closed down or metamorphosed, changing their names and locations. In a few cases, as in the two Massachusetts potteries, Dedham and Chelsea Keramic Art Works, the names represent separate phases in the career of a single potter—in this instance, Hugh Robertson.

ARKANSAS
Niloak Pottery: Benton

CALIFORNIA
Alberhill Pottery: Alberhill
Arequipa Pottery: Fairfax
J. A. Bauer Pottery: Los Angeles
California Faience: Berkeley
Grand Feu Art Pottery: Los Angeles
Halcyon Art Pottery: Halcyon
Markham Pottery: National City
Oakland Art Pottery: Oakland
Rhead Pottery: Santa Barbara
Robertson Pottery: Los Angeles, Hollywood
Roblin Art Pottery: San Francisco
Stockton Art Pottery: Stockton
Valentien Pottery: San Diego
Walrich Pottery: Berkeley

COLORADO
Denver China and Pottery: Denver
Van Briggle Pottery: Colorado Springs
White Pottery: Denver

CONNECTICUT
Wannopee Pottery: New Milford

ILLINOIS
Chicago Terra Cotta Works: Chicago
Norse Pottery: Rockford
Northwestern Terra Cotta: Chicago
Pauline Pottery: Chicago
Teco Pottery: Terra Cotta

INDIANA
Overbeck Pottery: Cambridge City

IOWA
Shawsheen Pottery: Mason City

KENTUCKY
Kenton Hills Porcelains: Erlanger

LOUISIANA
New Orleans Art Pottery: New Orleans
Newcomb Pottery: New Orleans

MARYLAND
Edwin Bennett Pottery: Baltimore

MASSACHUSETTS
Chelsea Keramic Art Works: Chelsea
Dedham Pottery: Dedham
Grueby Pottery: Boston
Low Art Tile Works: Chelsea
Marblehead Pottery: Marblehead
Merrimac Pottery: Newburyport
Paul Revere Pottery: Boston, Brighton
Shawsheen Pottery: Billerica
Walley Pottery: West Sterling

MICHIGAN
Markham Pottery: Ann Arbor
Pewabic Pottery: Detroit

MISSISSIPPI
Biloxi Art Pottery: Biloxi

MISSOURI
University City Pottery: University City

NEW HAMPSHIRE
Hampshire Pottery: Keene

NEW JERSEY
Clifton Art Pottery: Newark
Cook Pottery: Trenton
Fulper Pottery: Flemington
Poillon Pottery: Woodbridge
Volkmar Kilns: Metuchen

NEW YORK
American Art Ceramic Company: Corona
Brush Guild: New York City
Buffalo Pottery: Buffalo
Byrdcliffe Pottery: Woodstock
Corona Pottery: Corona
Durant Kilns: Bedford Village
Faience Manufacturing Company: Greenpoint
Graham Pottery: Brooklyn
Halm Art Pottery: Sandy Hill
Jervis Pottery: Oyster Bay
Kiss Art Pottery: Sag Harbor
Middle Lane Pottery: East Hampton, Westhampton
Odell & Booth Brothers: Tarrytown
Robineau Pottery: Syracuse
Tiffany Pottery: Corona
Volkmar Pottery: Tremont, Corona

OHIO
Arc-En-Ciel Pottery: Zanesville
Avon Pottery: Cincinnati
Cambridge Art Pottery: Cambridge
Cincinnati Art Pottery: Cincinnati
Clewell Metal Art: Canton
Coultry Pottery: Cincinnati
Cowan Pottery: Cleveland, Rocky River
Craven Art Pottery: East Liverpool
Dallas Pottery: Cincinnati
Dayton Porcelain Works: Dayton
Wm. Dell Pottery: Cincinnati
Etruscan Antique Art Works: Sebring
Faience Pottery: Zanesville
Florentine Pottery: Chillicothe
Lonhuda Pottery: Steubenville
Losanti: Cincinnati
J. W. McCoy Pottery: Roseville, Zanesville
Matt Morgan Art Pottery: Cincinnati
Miami Pottery: Dayton
Nielson Pottery: Zanesville
Oakwood Art Pottery: Wellsville
Oakwood Pottery: Dayton
Oakwood Pottery Company: East Liverpool
J. B. Owens Pottery: Zanesville
Peters and Reed Pottery: Zanesville
A. Radford Pottery: Tiffin, Zanesville
Rookwood Pottery: Cincinnati
Roseville Pottery: Zanesville
Trentvale Pottery: East Liverpool
C. B. Upjohn Pottery: Zanesville
Vance/Avon Faience: Tiltonville
Weller Pottery: Zanesville
H. A. Weller Art Pottery: Zanesville
T. J. Wheatley & Company: Cincinnati
Wheatley Pottery Company: Cincinnati
Zanesville Art Pottery: Zanesville

PENNSYLVANIA
Enfield Pottery: Laverock
Rose Valley Pottery: Rose Valley

TENNESSEE
Nashville Art Pottery: Nashville

VIRGINIA
Massanetta Art Pottery: Harrisonburg

WEST VIRGINIA
Lessell Art Ware: Parkersburg
A. Radford Pottery: Clarksburg
Sinclair Art Pottery: Chester
Vance/Avon Faience: Wheeling

WISCONSIN
American/Edgerton Art Clay Works: Edgerton
Edgerton Pottery: Edgerton
Frackelton Pottery: Milwaukee
Norse Pottery: Edgerton
Pauline Pottery: Edgerton

86 / ART POTTERY

An example of late, mass-produced art pottery is this lamp and shade with stained-glass inserts from the Fulper Pottery in New Jersey.

The green mat glaze, a staple of nearly every art pottery, is varied with a silvery gray patina in a vase from the Teco Pottery in Illinois.

pottery. But he never did. Meanwhile, the original pottery continued under new management until 1914, but without Doat, Rhead and Robineau as teachers.

Besides Robineau, two other women influenced the closing years of the art pottery movement. They were Mary Chase Perry, founder of the Pewabic Pottery in Detroit, and Mrs. James J. Storrow, a wealthy Bostonian who built and operated the Paul Revere Pottery for a group of immigrant girls just out of school who met on Saturday nights to read to one another and learn useful crafts. Mrs. Storrow was their patron, their club was called the S.E.G.—Saturday Evening Girls—and those initials identify much of their pottery.

Mary Chase Perry founded Pewabic in 1903 and for several years made hand-crafted earthenware decorated with the popular mat glazes of the day. But gradually she added more sophisticated factory-style equipment—a blunger to churn clay, a filter press to squeeze out water and a pugmill to knead and cut the clay. With this equipment she began to produce a clay body that was a cross between earthenware and porcelain and could be used for either mat or high-glaze finishes. Her crowning achievement was a type of pottery decorated with iridescent, dripping glazes on simply shaped forms. This is the Pewabic product most in demand, and it turns up fairly regularly because Perry—who became Mrs. William Stratton in 1918—continued working until her death at the age of 94 in 1961.

Mrs. Storrow's Paul Revere Pottery, first known as the Bowl Shop, eventually had four kilns and employed between 14 and 20 young women. Its products were inexpensive; a small Paul Revere vase could be purchased for as little as 75 cents. The marks S.E.G. and Paul Revere appear on the bottom of such objects as lamp bases, book ends, paperweights, inkwells and tea sets. For a time, during World War I, when European

Two relatively recent examples of art pottery, both of them commercially produced by Roseville, are a rose-patterned basket vase from the early 1940s and a blackberry-patterned vase from 1933.

sources of materials were cut off, the Saturday Evening Girls even made pottery heads for doll manufacturers.

This more-or-less chronological account of the art pottery movement touches only those potteries that represent the mainstream. Off on countless tributaries gifted potters plied their craft, some more successfully and for longer periods than others.

Most collectors, myself included, enter the field at its historical conclusion. They collect examples of art pottery made in the 1940s and 1950s by such big industrial art potteries as Roseville and Weller, which managed to keep going long after the movement had peaked. Much of this later ware is readily found and easily identifiable, for by that time the big potteries had standardized their markings. Also, most of it is inexpensive.

I still have a lavender-pink Weller casserole that I purchased in a Vermont thrift shop for 50 cents in 1969. It is "late" Weller and clearly utilitarian. The rest of my collection puts it to shame, but I keep it because it was the piece that piqued my curiosity and started me off on a fascinating hobby.

For related material, see the articles on Belleek, Bennington Pottery, Lalique and Tiffany Glass in separate volumes of The Encyclopedia of Collectibles.

MUSEUMS

Cincinnati Art Museum
Cincinnati, Ohio 45202

Chicago Historical Society
Chicago, Illinois 60614

Everson Museum of Art
Syracuse, New York 13202

Freer Gallery of Art
Washington, D.C. 20560

The Metropolitan Museum of Art
New York, New York 10028

Museum of Fine Arts
Boston, Massachusetts 02115

National Museum of History and Technology
Smithsonian Institution
Washington, D.C. 20560

The Newark Museum
Newark, New Jersey 07101

Zanesville Art Center
Zanesville, Ohio 43701

BOOKS

Arnest, Barbara M., ed., *Van Briggle Pottery: The Early Years.* Colorado Springs, Fine Arts Center, 1975.

Blasberg, Robert W., *George E. Ohr and His Biloxi Art Pottery.* J. W. Carpenter, 1973.

Clark, Robert J., ed., *The Arts and Crafts Movement in America.* Princeton University Art Museum, 1972.

Evans, Paul, *Art Pottery of the United States.* Charles Scribner's Sons, 1974.

Hawes, Lloyd E., *The Dedham Pottery and the Earlier Robertson's Chelsea Potteries.* Dedham Historical Society, 1968.

Henzke, Lucile, *American Art Pottery.* Thomas Nelson, Inc., 1970.

Huxford, Sharon and Bob, *The Collector's Encyclopedia of Roseville Pottery.* Collector Books, 1976.

Kovel, Ralph and Terry, *Kovels' Collector's Guide to American Art Pottery.* Crown Publishers Inc., 1974.

Peck, Herbert, *The Book of Rookwood Pottery.* Bonanza Books, 1968.

Purviance, Louise and Evan, and Norris Schneider: *Roseville Art Pottery in Color.* Wallace-Homestead Book Company, 1976.
Weller Art Pottery in Color. Wallace-Homestead Book Company, 1971.

40th Congress 2nd Session
United States of America.
House of Representatives
February 24th, 1868.

Resolved, "That Andrew Johnson, President of the United States, be impeached of High Crimes and Misdemeanors in office."

_____ Clerk   Schuyler Colfax, Speaker

Autographs
Handwritten Witnesses to History

You might say that I have been collecting autographs all my life. Like a lot of youngsters, I used to hang around stadium locker rooms, badgering baseball players and prize fighters for their signatures as they emerged. Most collectors begin the same way, simply by asking notable people for their autographs. But I did not become a serious collector until after I was graduated from college. In the half century since, the fascination has never worn off, for handwritten words and names tell a story much more vividly than printed ones. The stories that keep me searching are those associated with American political history, which comes alive in the original material written by its participants.

My first goal was to get examples of the handwriting of all the Presidents, bought in the form of "clipped signatures," that is, signatures that have been cut off documents or letters. These are not overly difficult to

Although Nathaniel E. Stein is a semiretired stockbroker, he has not yet retired from autograph collecting. His collection of American historical autographs is one of the best in the country.

find now because they were widely sold during the 19th Century, when many American families kept autograph albums on display on a parlor table. Because only the signature was regarded as worth collecting for display, stories are common about people who obtained an entire letter written by Abraham Lincoln and discarded everything but the signature. Since most serious collectors of today shun these clipped signatures and instead look for complete documents or letters, beginning collectors can often pick them up quite inexpensively.

Though I, too, soon looked for complete letters and manuscripts, I expanded my collection of clipped signatures of the Presidents so that it would be complete through John F. Kennedy. Each one has been framed along with the official bronze medallion of the President, which can be purchased from the U.S. Mint. The collection hangs on two walls of my living room, where it makes an attractive display.

President Andrew Johnson took from official files—and gave to a friend—the 1868 Congressional resolution that impeached him.

Collectors of Presidential autographs always prefer those written while a President was in office, but sometimes they are difficult to find. James A. Garfield's signature is particularly rare because he was in office less than seven months. He was inaugurated on March 4, 1881, but was shot on July 2 by a frustrated job-seeker, and died of the wound on September 19. The assassin's name was Charles J. Guiteau, and I managed to find his confession of the shooting along with the signatures, on individual cards, of each member of the jury that tried him. I also have one of the tickets that admitted the public to the trial.

Even rarer is the signature of President William Henry Harrison, who was the first President to die while in office. He was 68 when he was inaugurated, on March 4,

A "clipped signature," cut from a letter or document, is displayed with a medallion of President William Howard Taft.

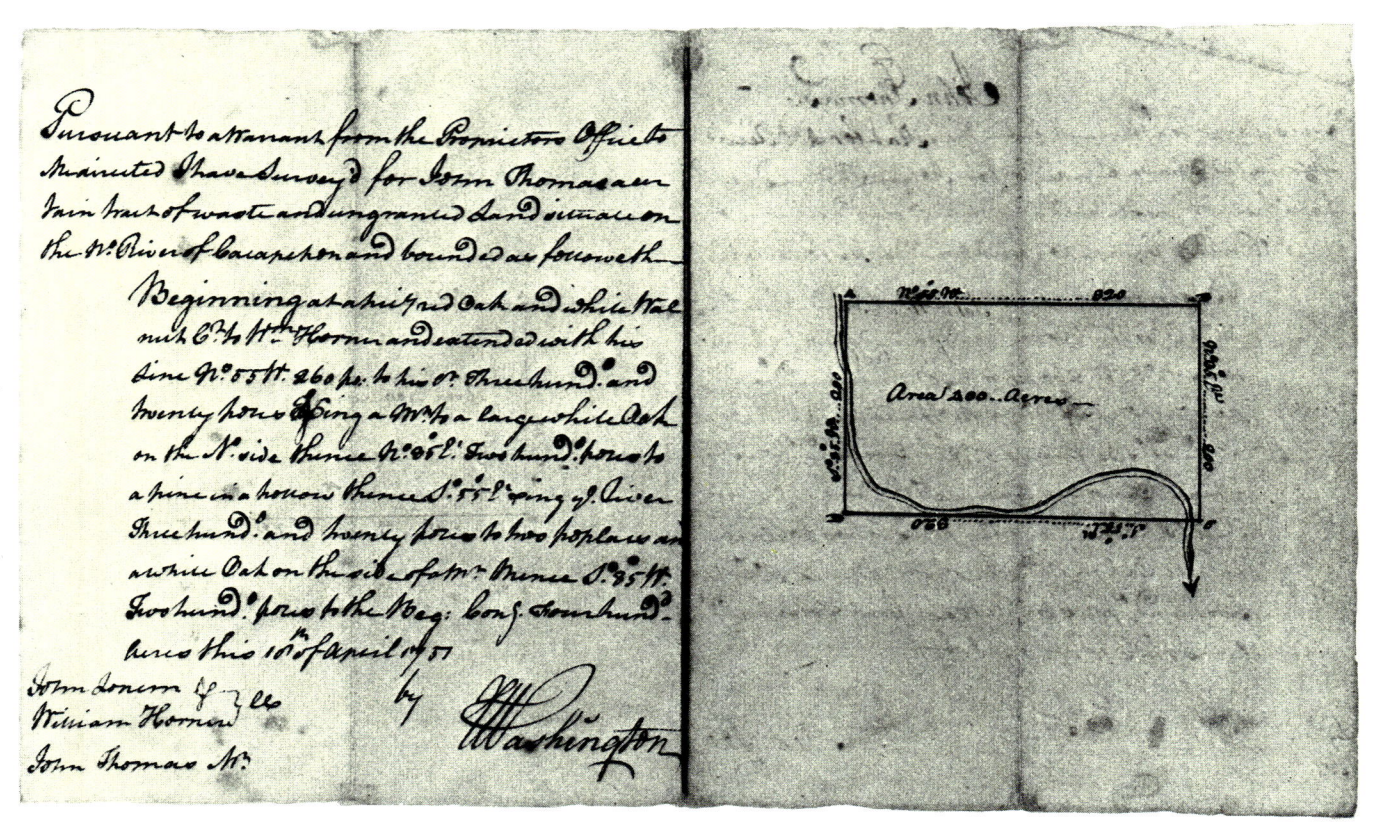

George Washington's first job as a surveyor in Virginia produced this handwritten description of a piece of land on the Cacapon River.

Signed by Washington when he was only 19, the document includes, as a bonus for the collector, a meticulously hand-drawn map.

1841, and he caught cold at the ceremony and died one month later of pneumonia. I have never seen a letter written by him during that month, but I managed to find a letter written while he was President-elect. I also found a document signed by him during his brief term in office—a paper permitting a ship to clear port, signed just five days after his inauguration. It is also signed, as a bonus, by Daniel Webster, who was then Secretary of State *(page 95)*.

My efforts to obtain examples of handwriting by all the Presidents represent a typical form of collecting: assembling autographs in sets. Some collectors try to get all the signers of the Declaration of Independence or all the Justices of the Supreme Court, or all the Nobel Prize winners. Because my own interests are financial—I am a stockbroker—I have tried to compile one other Presidential set, a collection of canceled checks, one for each President. That was a challenge; 22 years elapsed before I had a set from Washington to Franklin Roosevelt. And when the collection was finally completed, a New York bank heard about it and made me such a good offer for it that I sold the set.

I still collect autographed checks, and I have a few that I am especially fond of. One is a check for $18,000 authorized to be given to the Marquis de Lafayette by the U.S. Congress in gratitude for his services during the American Revolution *(page 94)*.

Checks are not my only specialty. The most popular form of autograph is probably a signed letter handwritten by someone of interest. After that comes a signed document, such as a will or a deed; a book with the owner's signature on the flyleaf; or an autographed photograph. I managed to find fascinating examples of all four. One is a chatty letter written by Martha Washington to her parish minister, commenting on her husband's health and remarking on how well she and Mr. Washington were able to hear since Dr. Rush had cleaned out their ears. As in most of Mrs. Washington's letters, the spelling is atrocious; when she needed to correspond with someone important, she usually got her husband to write the letter for her.

My prize example of a signed document is the labored signature of Barbara Fritchie, witnessing what is apparently the settlement of an estate. This obscure woman of Frederick, Maryland, is remembered only for her supposed defiance of Confederate General Stonewall Jackson during the Civil War, when she challenged him, in the words of John Greenleaf Whittier's poem, to

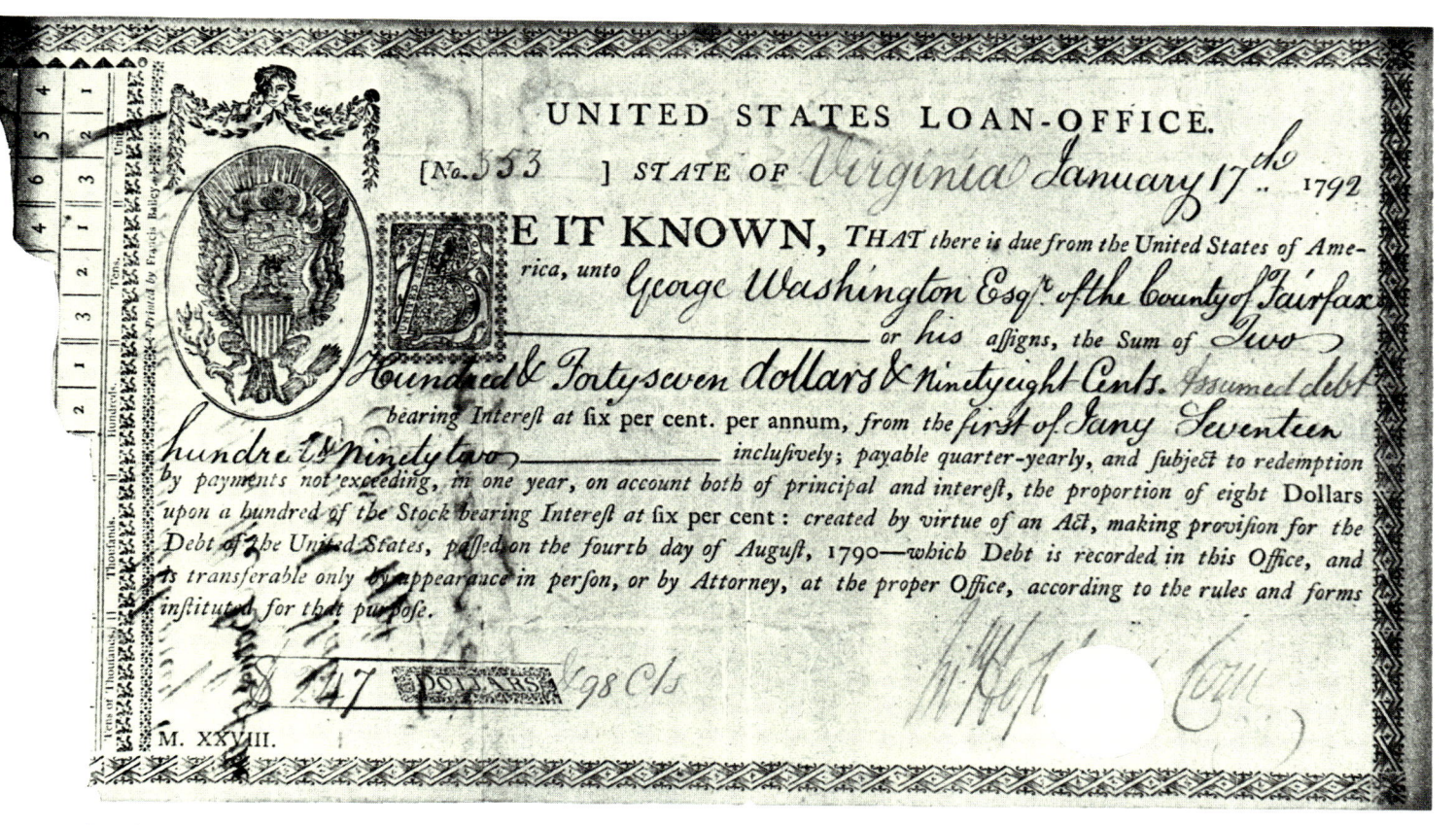

In 1792, the U.S. government paid a debt to former President Washington of $247.98; the document (above) was endorsed by Washington to his account in the U.S. Treasury in October 1794 (below). The hole in the document corner is a cancellation mark.

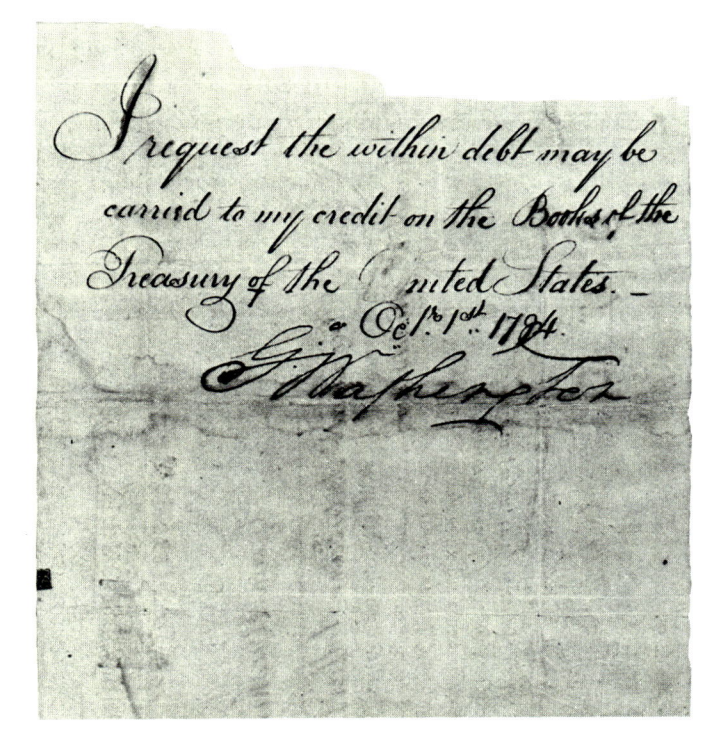

THE LANGUAGE OF AUTOGRAPHS

Autograph dealers use the following standard abbreviations to identify their catalogue offerings.

- **ADS**: autograph document signed. A receipt or check, written and signed by the same person
- **ALS**: autograph letter signed. A letter written and signed by the same person
- **AMs**: autograph manuscript. A handwritten but unsigned manuscript
- **AMsS**: autograph manuscript signed. A manuscript written and signed by the same person
- **ANS**: autograph note signed. A two- or three-line note, written and signed by the same person
- **APcS**: autograph postcard signed. A postcard written and signed by the same person
- **C**: card. A visiting card, usually signed by the person whose name is printed on it
- **DS**: document signed. A document typed or written by one person and signed by another
- **LS**: letter signed. A letter handwritten by one person but signed by another
- **Ms**: manuscript. Anything handwritten except a letter or document
- **TLS**: typed letter signed. A typewritten letter signed by the sender

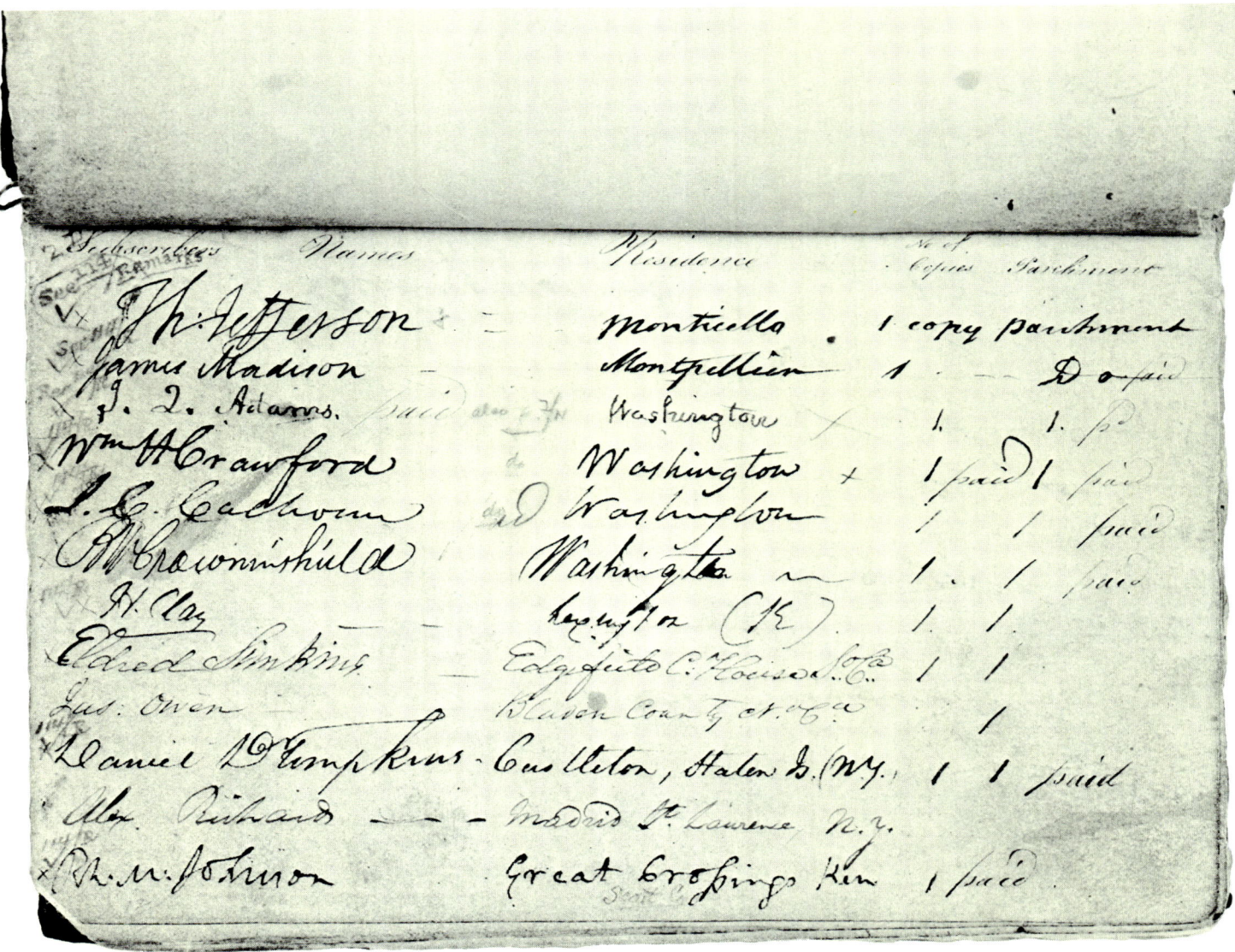

When facsimiles of the Declaration of Independence were sold in the early 1800s, subscribers wrote their names and addresses in an order book and specified parchment or paper copies. Thomas Jefferson's signature is first, but not necessarily the most valuable on this page.

"shoot, if you must, this old gray head." Her autograph is extremely rare. She was probably no more than semiliterate, and she never signed more than a half dozen documents during her entire life.

To round out my examples of autograph categories, I have a textbook on stenography that had been bought by Nathan Hale at third hand, if the inscription on the title page is to be trusted. Two other names preceded Hale's. He added the date of purchase: November 12, 1774. He was at the time a 19-year-old school teacher in Connecticut, just out of Yale University. Less than two years later he was captured and hanged by the British in New York as a spy.

I also have an extremely rare *carte de visite* signed by Abraham Lincoln. *Cartes de visite* were small photographs mounted on cardboard and used as calling cards in the 1860s, when photographs were still a novelty. Lincoln's is unusually desirable, partly because it was made by the famous Civil War photographer, Mathew Brady, but mainly because, in the space provided for the caller's name—which was often printed—Lincoln has written his signature.

The Lincoln *carte de visite*, like many other autographs, is supplemented by related memorabilia: Lincoln campaign badges, one of them bearing his photograph; a piece of the flag that decorated the box in Ford's Theater where he was sitting when John Wilkes Booth shot him; and the first reward poster to be printed after the shooting, promising a generous sum for the apprehension of the assassin. A few years ago I

> John Adams President of the United States of America
>
> To John Quincy Adams — Greeting
>
> Reposing especial Trust and Confidence in your Integrity, Prudence and Ability, I have nominated and by and with the advice and consent of the Senate do appoint you the said John Quincy Adams Minister Plenipotentiary for the United States of America at the Court of His Majesty the King of Prussia, authorizing you hereby to do and perform all such Matters and Things as to the said Place or Office doth appertain, or as may be duly given you in charge hereafter, and the said Office to hold and exercise during the pleasure of the President of the United States for the time being.
>
> In Testimony whereof I have caused the Seal of the United States to be hereunto affixed. Given under my hand at the city of Philadelphia the First day of June in the year of our Lord one thousand seven hundred and ninety seven, and of the Independence of the United States of America the Twenty first.
>
> John Adams
>
> By the President of the United States
>
> Timothy Pickering, Secretary of State

A 1797 document bearing the signature of President John Adams appoints his 30-year-old son, John Quincy, United States minister to Prussia. The younger Adams had been in the diplomatic service since his teens, and later became President himself.

put together a little exhibition of this material in the window of my brokerage office on Lincoln's birthday. As I went out to lunch I noticed a passerby look at the Booth poster and ask his companion, "Are they still looking for him?"

In addition to the four main types of autographs, all of which bear actual signatures, collectors also seek another type: manuscripts handwritten by persons of interest, whether signed or not. In this group are not only early versions of literary works such as essays and poems, but also drafts of speeches. The manuscript of a speech I especially wanted led me on one of my longest chases—and it is not over yet. This is an early draft of Washington's first inaugural address, written in his own hand. It was cut up in the 19th Century by Jared Sparks, an early biographer of Washington who was able to borrow all of the papers in the Washington family. Sparks, who was nothing if not accommodating, passed out the pieces to people who wanted samples of Washington's handwriting. Until I started to put it together, it had never been reassembled. Over the years I bought bits and pieces of it until I now have 23 of the manuscript's 32 pages. Every major U.S. autograph dealer knows by now that I am in the market for the rest—one dealer recently called me to offer a segment containing just four words.

Although I depend on book and autograph dealers to keep me informed of things they can provide, I still find a lot of material on my own. Success depends greatly on luck. But luck comes most often to those who know where to look, whether they are searching for famous rarities or assembling autographs that attract them alone. One rule to remember is that autographs are parts of something else—documents, letters, books, photographs—and thus looking for the something else is a good way to start. Piles of old photographs, for example, are commonly found in flea markets at fairly low prices; many, like the Lincoln *carte de visite,* bear famous signatures.

The obvious place to hunt for books, of course, is bookshops. One day, during a trip to the Edinburgh Music Festival in the autumn of 1968, I went window-shopping down Princes Street and stepped into an antiquarian bookstore. The proprietor asked me if I was interested in anything special, and when I told him I collected old manuscripts and documents dealing with American history, he took down a newspaper-wrapped bundle from a top shelf. It contained a book printed in 1793 for the Tontine Coffee House Society, the first group of Americans to deal in securities, and the forerunner of the New York Stock Exchange. The book listed all the members of the society, and beside many of the names were the members' signatures. Included are such famous names in New York history as Van Rensselaer, Astor and Stewart.

Old furniture may seem to be an unlikely source of autographs, but once you think about it you realize that bureaus, chests and desks are repositories for papers of all kinds. A friend of mine happened to buy an antique chest at a Virginia flea market, and his purchase led to one of the most exciting finds I ever made. When the chest was put up for sale no one had bothered to clean out the drawers. And in one was a cache of 300 to 400 handwritten pages of notes, letters and articles on the Virginia Declaration of Rights—the model for the Bill of Rights of the U.S. Constitution—apparently in the hand of George Mason, the Tidewater plantation owner who wrote them. I examined this material, as it happened, sitting in a pew of the old Pohick church, not far from Mason's home. When I finished and looked up, my hair nearly stood on end; there on the brass plate identifying the pew's owner was the name George Mason. Eventually I sold these papers for inclusion in the archives of the restored Mason home.

Like the Mason material, some autographs come to me through people who know me or know about my interest. On a trip to Mexico several years ago, I heard about and acquired—from the widow of a professor at the University of Mexico—a famous letter, written by a Massachusetts man to Abraham Lincoln, pleading for clemency for a young drummer boy who had been sentenced to death for falling asleep at his post. Across the back of the letter Lincoln had scrawled, "Let the boy be pardoned, A. Lincoln."

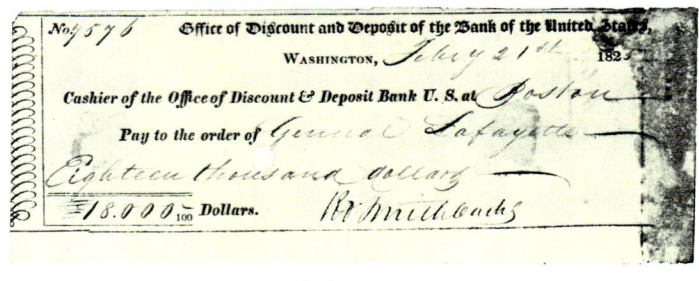

When Congress awarded the Marquis de Lafayette an $18,000 check (top) for his services in the Revolution, the Marquis inadvertently made a wry comment on world conditions with his endorsement (above)—he deposited the money in a safe place, a London bank.

Not every collectible autograph is that of a hero. In the letter shown above, the renegade American military commander Benedict Arnold, then living in London, petitions King George for a military appointment, citing his past services to the Crown.

Surprisingly fascinating autographs may be made available by any occasion that disposes of half-forgotten papers—receipts, business letters, personal notes. Such items, often valuable, turn up at the auctions of the household goods of an aged, once-prominent person, either inside drawers, like the George Mason papers, or among books and pictures. They may also surface from dusty files of a public agency or private company when the organization is closed down or absorbed by another.

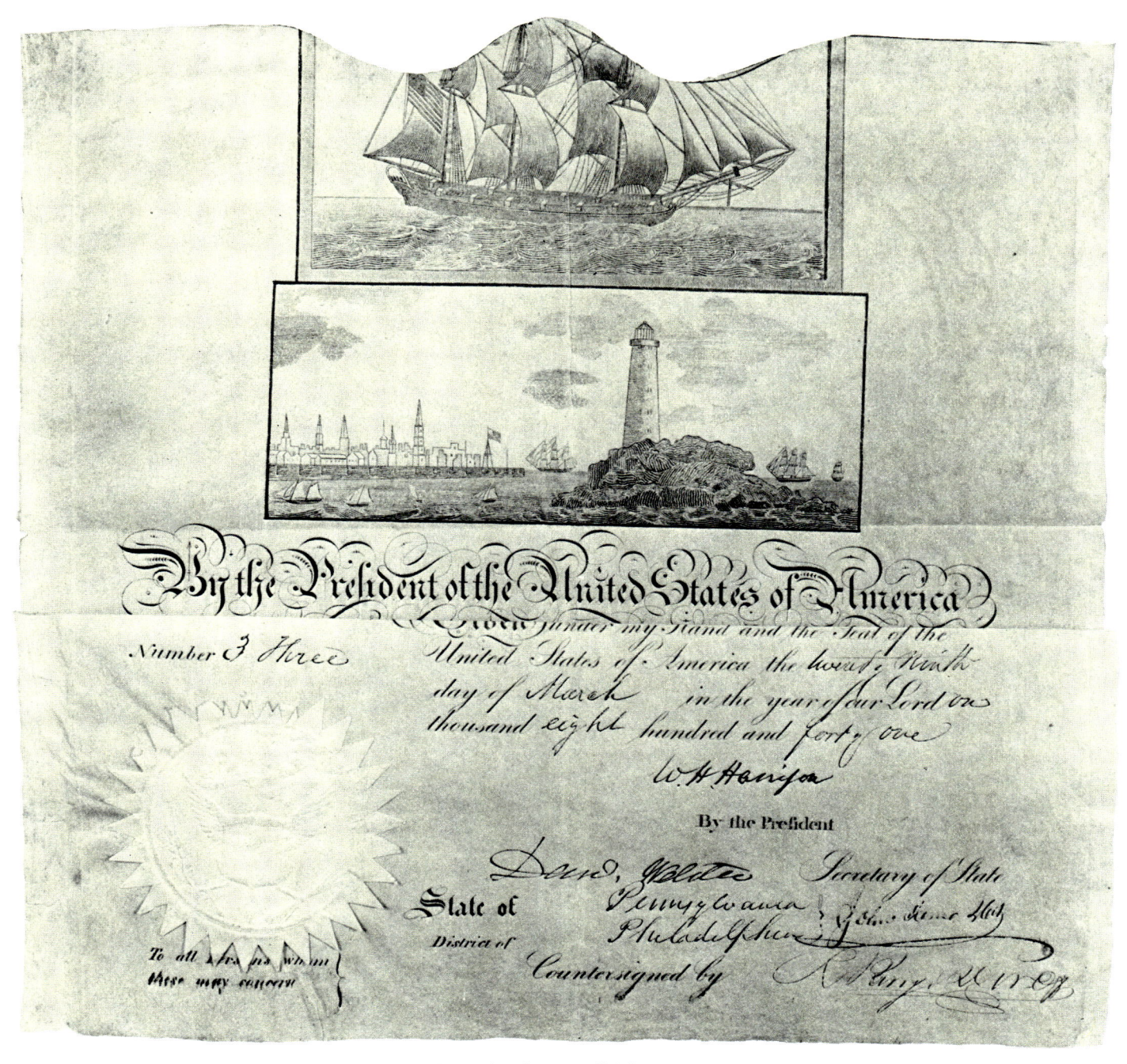

President William Henry Harrison, who died 30 days after his inauguration, left behind few autographs made in office. His rare official signature is on a routine document giving a vessel permission to leave port. It is also signed by Secretary of State Daniel Webster.

Such an event led to an unusual find that fitted my old interest in sports autographs, which have fascinated me ever since I was a child. I received a call from the secretary to brewery owner Jacob Ruppert at the time Ruppert sold the New York Yankees to Dan Topping. Going through the Ruppert files, the secretary had put together a collection of checks and contracts signed by such baseball giants as Babe Ruth, Lou Gehrig and Leo Durocher. I bought them all for $500 and eventually resold them to Sports Illustrated, which donated them to the Baseball Hall of Fame in Cooperstown, New York.

During my half century of collecting, I have seen the prices of important historical manuscripts and documents rise sharply, as more and more people and institutions have become interested in acquiring them. Few individuals can hope to put together autograph collections as impressive as those that were amassed in the last century, or even when I began. Fortunately, however,

96 / AUTOGRAPHS

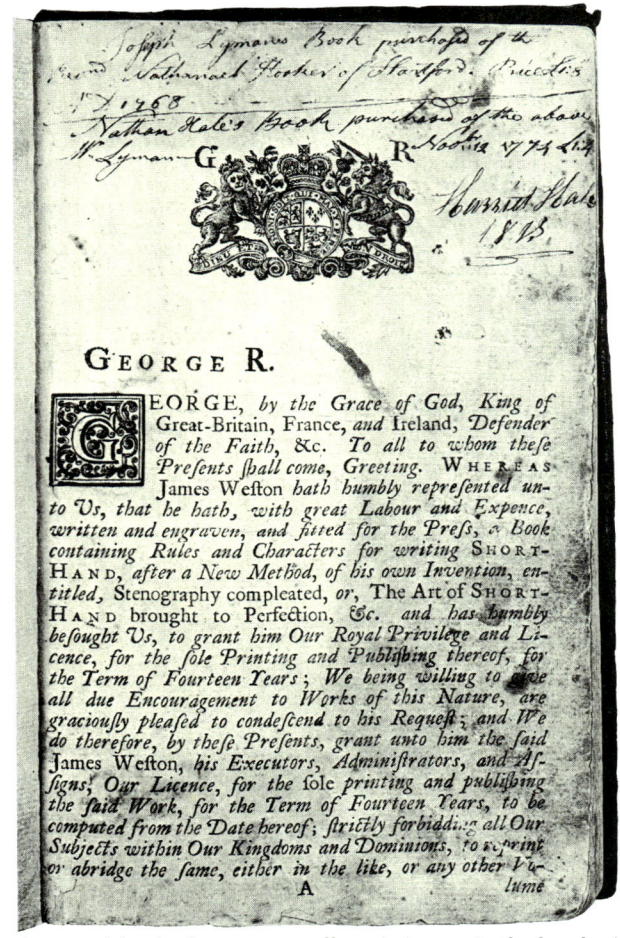

Books owned by the famous are collector's items. As the handwritten note attests, patriot Nathan Hale owned this shorthand book.

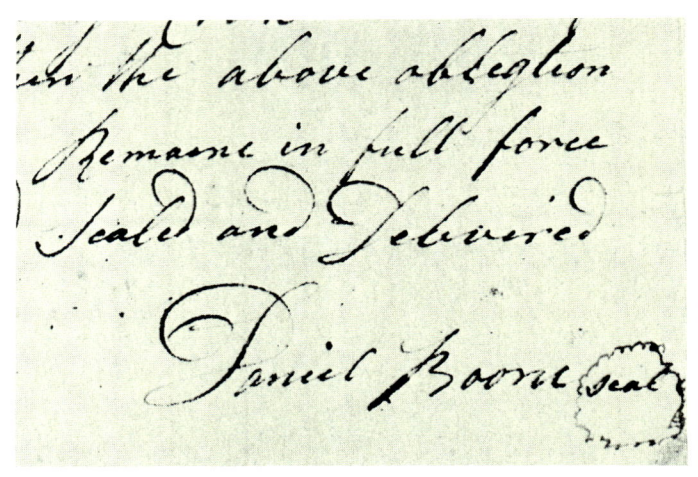

A fragment of Daniel Boone's handwriting indicates that the famous wilderness scout was not as illiterate as generally supposed.

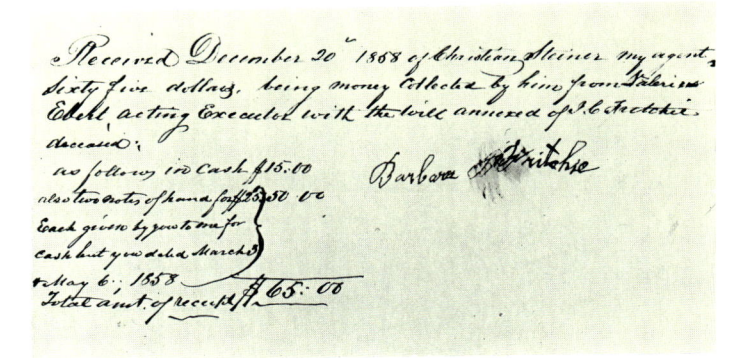

The legendary Barbara Fritchie of Civil War fame was also a real person who signed this receipt for $65, in settlement of an estate.

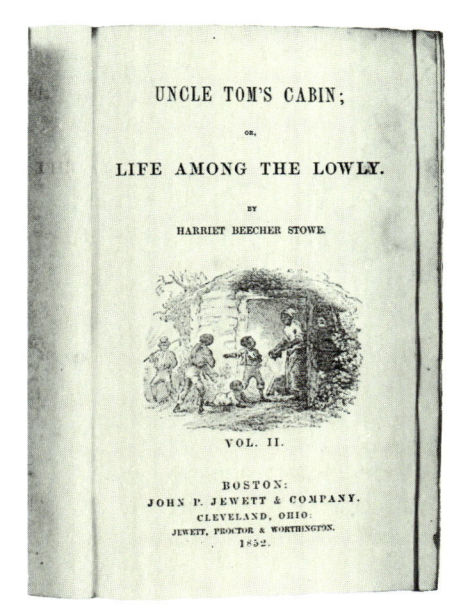

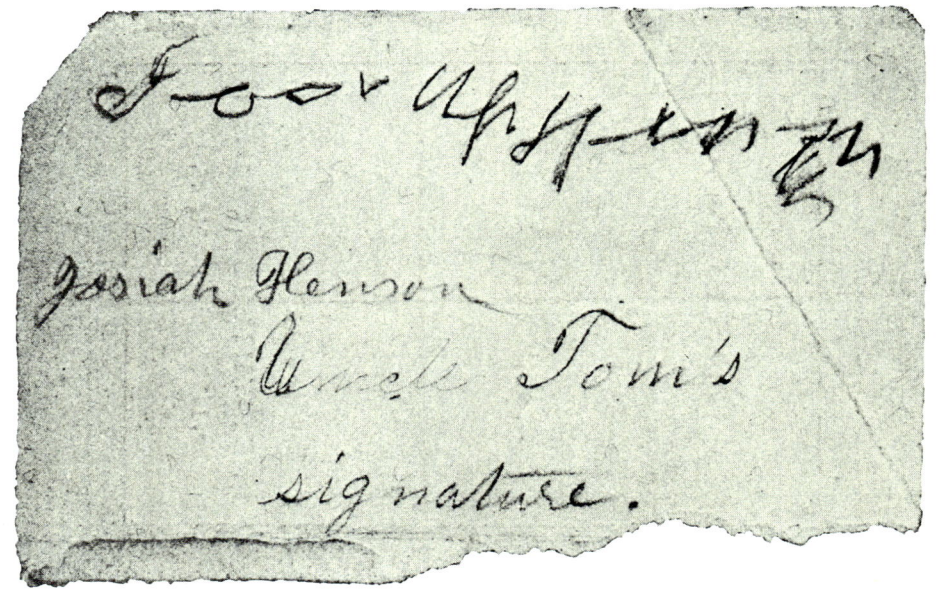

Written laboriously late in life under the tutelage of Harriet Beecher Stowe, the signature of Josiah Henson, the original "Tom" of "Uncle Tom's Cabin," is pasted on the front endpaper of Mrs. Stowe's copy of the first edition of her famous novel, published in 1852.

Perhaps the best-known autograph in America—and quite rare—is the signature of John Hancock, as exuberant on this lottery ticket as on the Declaration of Independence.

Master Forger

The most skillful autograph forger of this century, according to New York authority Charles Hamilton, was probably Joseph Cosey, who operated in New York City in the 1930s. Cosey obtained vintage paper for the expertly imitated signatures, and he victimized dealers by pretending to offer his forgeries for appraisal only, never claiming they were genuine.

Cosey's specialty was the handwriting of Abraham Lincoln, but he also forged signatures of Alexander Hamilton, Thomas Jefferson and Edgar Allan Poe, among others. Below, along with a genuine signature of Benjamin Franklin *(bottom)*, is an example of Cosey's handiwork. He gave himself away by copying a 1757 Franklin document, and presenting it as one written 30 years later, when Franklin was an old man. Franklin's real signature at that time—crabbed and shaky—vividly betrayed his age.

A FORGED FRANKLIN SIGNATURE

A REAL ONE

A Memorable Surrender

Two gems from Nathaniel Stein's autograph collection are this document and a picture that goes with it. The document is the moving General Order No. 9, in which Confederate General Robert E. Lee informs his officers and troops of the surrender at Appomattox Courthouse, Virginia, bringing the Civil War to an end. Displayed with General Order No. 9 is an original drawing of the surrender scene (far right), done by the artist Alfred Waud on commission from *Harper's Weekly*.

The order is one of several drafted by Lee's aides for his approval. This one, which Lee signed, is dated "Headquarters of the Army of No. Virginia, 10th April, 1865" and explains with dignity the circumstances that forced the surrender. It concludes with a tribute to those who fought under his command:

"With an increasing admiration for your constancy and devotion to your country and a grateful remembrance of your kind and generous consideration of myself, I bid you all an affectionate farewell.
R. E. Lee Genl"

Waud, who is thought to have been present when the surrender was signed, depicted the scene in a way that at the time drew criticism from the victors. Lee is shown in the center of the composition, his figure bathed in a stream of overhead light, while Grant is seated in shadow at the right. Many people felt that Grant should have been made the central figure. Today, however, Waud's drawing is a valuable historical reference. When McLean House, where the surrender took place, was restored as a national monument in the 1940s, researchers used his drawing as a guide in reconstructing the appearance of the room and arranging furnishings to replace the originals, long since carried off as souvenirs.

Lee's signature on "General Order No. 9" is considered his best.

---

there is still a great deal of material that is available for collectors of modest means.

When people ask me how to go about starting an autograph collection, I tell them to specialize—to pick out some category of profession or history, such as Civil War generals, state governors, artists or movie stars, and seek letters, manuscripts, documents and signatures of the people who fit that category. The category itself helps to tell you where to look. Civil War material, for example, is not as likely to turn up at a country auction in North Dakota as it is in Virginia or Massachusetts, while artists' signatures are sure to be more plentiful in and around cities where galleries and studios are concentrated.

But do not overlook some obvious sources of interesting autographs of modest cash value. One New York department store successfully sold autographs for more than 30 years at prices from $7.50 to $3,500. And the individual dealers who specialize in autographs do not limit their clientele to the wealthy. The price depends on a variety of factors—clipped signatures are less expensive than letters and documents, for example. One gallery often sells autographs in lots of 10 to 20 at reasonable prices; in 1977 it offered 19-piece portfolios of signed photographs of a galaxy of movie stars for $160. Another dealer's catalogue listed material signed by Ernest Hemingway for $75, P. T. Barnum for $20, Orville Wright for $75, Henry Wadsworth Longfellow for $20 and Admiral Horatio Nelson for $100.

Since categories seem to go in and out of fashion, bargain-hunting collectors look for groups that are now out rather than in. Signatures of wartime figures, for example, are always popular, but their value depends on

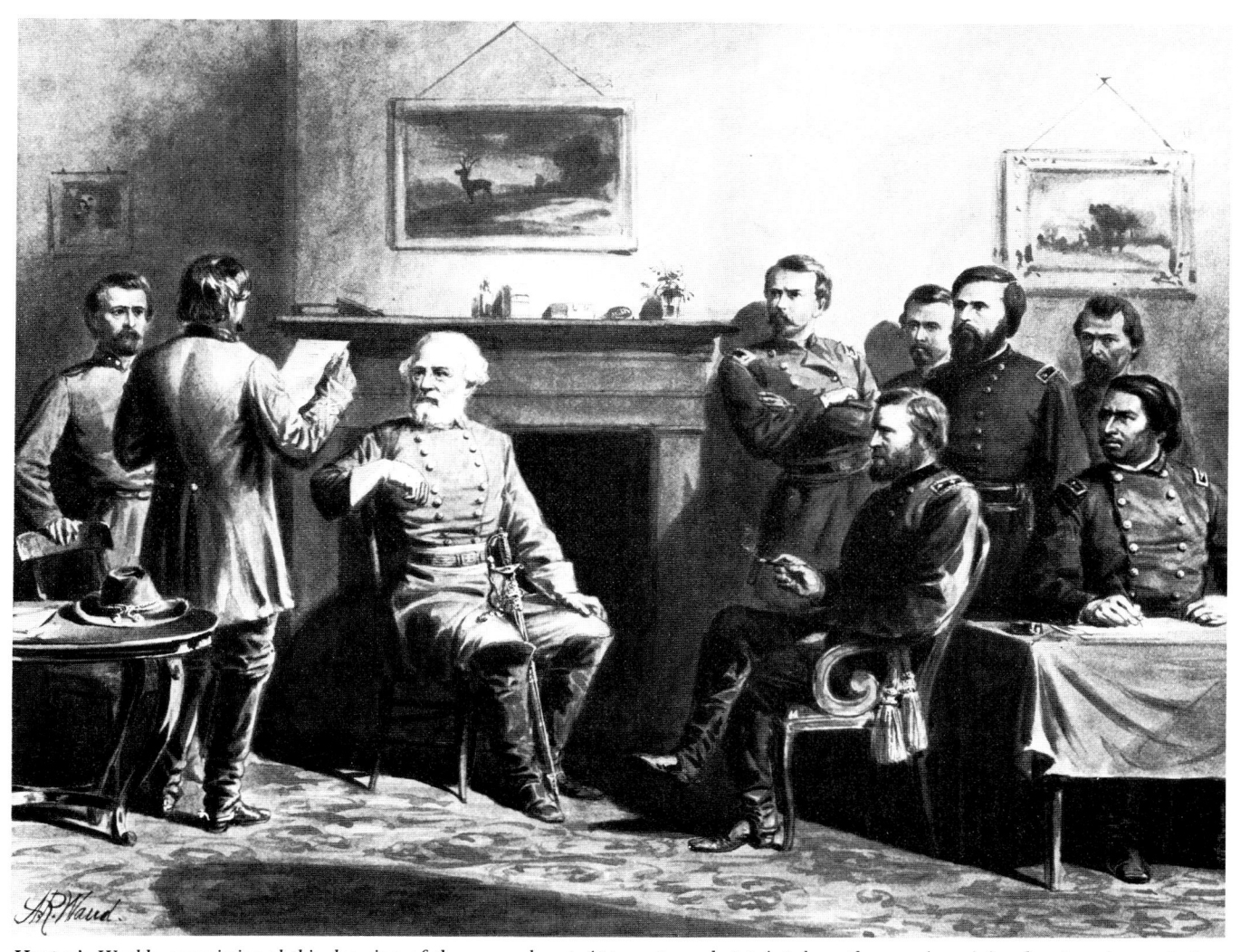

Harper's Weekly commissioned this drawing of the surrender at Appomattox—but printed another version giving less prominence to Lee.

which war the signer was in. World War II autographs and memorabilia were much in demand during the 1970s but World War I was neglected, and signatures of its admirals, generals and statesmen were readily obtainable at low prices. Even less in vogue was the Spanish-American War, and autographs of Admiral George Dewey, General Leonard Wood and other participants could be bought for less than $100. Interest in the Civil War never flags, but there is so much material from this period antedating the typewriter that letters signed by all the generals on both sides were selling at moderate prices—provided they were dated before or after the war years of 1860-1865. Letters written while the fighting continued have always been prized.

Fashion—or snobbery—can also be detected in the varying values of musicians' and artists' autographs. The interest in Mozart is strong and international. Although he wrote many letters—pleading for money—one of his letters sold for $17,500 in 1975. Those of European modern painters were much sought after during the late 1970s, but autographs of Americans were not; as a result material signed by such famous artists as John Singer Sargent, Andrew Wyeth and Andy Warhol was relatively inexpensive. Among other categories with modest values were Nobel Prize winners, opera stars, U.S. Cabinet members and British Prime Ministers (letters signed by Robert Walpole or David Lloyd George went for less than $100). Movie stars' autographs varied in value, depending on the star—Joan Crawford's could be found for $10, but Clark Gable's commanded $75 and Rudolph Valentino's $100.

Understandably low in price have been the auto-

How a Novice Collector Set Out to Acquire Big-Name Autographs

Nick Hentoff was only 13 years old when, in 1973, he was given the first item in his autograph collection, a letter of General U. S. Grant. Like many collectors, he is particularly interested in American history, especially anecdotes and stories about historical figures. To supplement his autographs, he collects political cartoons, campaign posters and newspapers.

The first autograph he bought was a relatively inexpensive Franklin D. Roosevelt letter which he bid for in person at an auction. With the help of a relative he was able to purchase a coveted George Washington document, also signed by Thomas Jefferson, appointing George Gale Supervisor of the District of Maryland; it is one of his most prized possessions. Hentoff's Lincoln autograph *(below)*, more modestly priced, was purchased with money earned by working during summer vacations. While still a student, Hentoff went about his hobby methodically. He researched autographs he hoped to buy, reading auction catalogues, price lists and dealers' lists, and writing to dealers and other collectors. He located few autographs at flea markets and antique shows but found them a good source of related material such as posters and newspapers.

Outright purchases are necessarily limited for young collectors. Hentoff did not forget to use family connections to acquire signatures from famous people *(above, right)*. And many prize examples he gathered by simply asking. A few autographs came through correspondence with celebrities such as astronaut Buzz Aldrin *(below, left)*. And he got President Jimmy Carter's signature through a campaign worker Hentoff knew who asked the President to autograph one of his books. To go with this signature, he acquired a subway advertising card for the Carter campaign but, as he is careful to point out, he scrupulously waited until after the election to take it from the rack.

Hentoff wrote to astronaut Buzz Aldrin after reading his book, "Return to Earth," and in response got this valuable autograph.

Abraham Lincoln endorsed so many documents while in office that his signature is easy for novice collectors to find.

graphs of the most anonymous of American political leaders, the Vice Presidents. But even Presidents' signatures have been modestly priced, with a few exceptions. One of the exceptions is John F. Kennedy, who wrote few letters and had most documents signed by an automatic machine; one letter he did write when he was a Senator sold in 1977 for nearly $1,000. But such unusual material aside, the signature of nearly all Presidents since 1865 could be bought for $35 to $75 each.

It is even possible to get most of the signers of the Declaration of Independence—although one that probably will have to be left to the wealthy is the signature of Button Gwinnett, the Georgia pig farmer who apparently put his name to paper so infrequently that his autograph is worth between $30,000 and $50,000.

For related material, see the articles on Books, Dance Memorabilia, Detective Fiction, Jazz Memorabilia, Lindbergh Memorabilia, Menus, Movie Memorabilia, Opera Mementos and Theatrical Memorabilia in separate volumes of The Encyclopedia of Collectibles.

Through his father Nat Hentoff, a well-known jazz critic, young Hentoff added this star to his collection, an autograph of the great jazz singer, Billie Holiday, who was called Lady Day.

George Bernard Shaw thriftily used postcards in his voluminous correspondence. This one was written when GBS was 89.

LIBRARIES
Bancroft Library
Berkeley, California 94720

Bentley Historical Library
Ann Arbor, Michigan 48109

Huntington Library
San Marino, California 91108

The New York Public Library
New York, New York 10018

Newberry Library
Chicago, Illinois 60610

The Pierpont Morgan Library
New York, New York 10016

COLLECTORS ORGANIZATIONS
The Manuscript Society
1206 North Stoneman Avenue
No. 15
Alhambra, California 91801

Universal Autograph Collectors Club
P.O. Box 467-ACM
Rockville Centre, New York 11571

BOOKS
Hamilton, Charles, *Collecting Autographs and Manuscripts.* University of Oklahoma Press, 1970.

Patterson, Jerry E., *Autographs: A Collectors' Guide.* Crown Publishers, Inc., 1973.

Automobilia
Mementos of Early Motor Cars

Side by side with the hobby of collecting old automobiles (see *Cars* in a separate volume), Americans are also collecting automobilia—all of the equipment fastened to old cars or associated with them. This material naturally includes accessories, such as lamps, horns, name plates, hubcaps, radiator caps, license plates and club badges. But it also extends to a host of other kinds of material relating to automobiles—paintings, prints, photographs, advertisements, brochures, catalogues, books, jewelry, household items decorated with automobile designs and much, much more. With such a large field to choose from, many collectors elect to specialize—some very narrowly. There are people who collect only license plates or hubcaps and nothing else. My own collection, assembled

---
Collector Henry Austin Clark Jr., owner of the Long Island Automotive Museum, has been involved with automobiles since he was 12, when he helped rebuild a truck from parts found in a city dump.

---

over the last 30 years, is broad, covering almost every area of old-car memorabilia.

Old headlights and horns are among the more popular collectibles because they are such handsome objects. Today headlights are built in, horns are hidden under the hood, and neither is a thing of beauty when removed from its mounting. But the brass oil and gas lamps and the bulb horns of the old days were separate, demountable objects and many were well designed. Junkmen customarily removed them before cutting up a car and threw them into barrels to be sold for scrap brass. Occasionally a barrel of them survived this fate, and they still turn up in the automobilia market.

The horns especially are appealing. Not only are they handsome, but they make interesting noises. The old bulb horns give a harsh quack even when disconnected from the car. The others make their original sounds only while they are attached to a car of similar age. The "owooga" of the early electric horn gets louder as the car accelerates. And the exhaust horns, which use pressurized gases that are bypassed from the car's exhaust, make noises that range from melodious chimes to the shrill bleat of a steamboat whistle. After World War I,

most of the horns were electric. But one that was produced at that time was the last relic of an older, more romantic era: the bulb horn called the Testaphone *(page 105)*. It sounds several notes, each separately controlled, and can be made to play a tune. These horns were so often stolen that the mounting eventually was designed to allow the horn to slip off easily for removal to a more secure spot when the car was parked.

But esthetics—visual or aural—are only one consideration. Probably the most interesting items to all collectors of automobilia are those that identify the car, indicating its make, model or serial number. The most

Two very rare serial-number plates, cast from bronze, once identified an American-made Stevens-Duryea of about 1904, and a French-made Renault of about 1909.

Two of America's most famous cars are recalled by their radiator emblems. The 1912 Thomas Flyer uses as its theme the New York-to-Paris Race of 1908, which the Thomas won. It shows the 21,000-mile route followed by the racers around the world. The Stutz emblem, dating from about 1916, bears the name of the city where the cars were made until production ceased in 1935.

Five hubcaps from the days when only the wheel hub was covered include, clockwise from lower left, a 1914 White, from either a car or a light truck; a 1906 Mercedes, made by the Daimler Motor Works of Germany; a 1909 Simplex, a chain-driven car built until 1929; a 1905 Locomobile, the first American mass-produced car; and a cap from a 1936 Packard Twelve, a notable classic car.

Before radiators were hidden by grilles, radiator caps were distinctive. From left are: a Pontiac Indian head of about 1927; a 1917 Simplex car's Moto-Meter, which indicated engine temperature; a mechanic figurine sold for any car; and an automobile-club cap.

obvious such identification is the name plate, also called a radiator emblem because it was affixed at first directly to the radiator and later to the decorative shell that covered the radiator. It was part of most automobiles from the earliest days, before 1910, until World War II. The standard name plate was made of copper or brass, often with baked enamel between the letters. On many the brass was plated with nickel or chromium, but on early name plates it remained yellow.

Manufacturers did not provide emblems on every model, and the frequency of issue obviously affects the present value. Emblems that were produced only intermittently are particularly prized. Pierce-Arrow, for example, had a name plate in only one year: 1928. Some owners of the Pierce-Arrow, proud to be driving one of the aristocrats of motordom, decided to mount name plates of their own design, which usually included their own initials—and such added-on identification is much sought after today.

An identification with a serious purpose is the serial-number plate, generally fastened to the dashboard facing the front-seat passenger, but sometimes placed under the hood or on the engine side of the firewall partition that separates engine from passengers. This plate, etched on brass or aluminum, has the model and serial number of the car stamped on it, and sometimes the engine number as well. Junk dealers used to remove

This mahogany and brass dashboard coil box worked with a magneto generator to provide current for spark plugs. A buzzer—visible under the lifted cover—signaled the 1906 driver to switch to the "MAG," or magneto, setting to save wear on the battery.

AUTOMOBILIA / 105

These brass lamps from pre-1913 autos were nonelectric, making matches mandatory equipment. Both the acetylene gas lamp (left) and the kerosene lamp (right) were mounted, one on each side, at the windshield base. The acetylene lamp threw a beam about 200 yards.

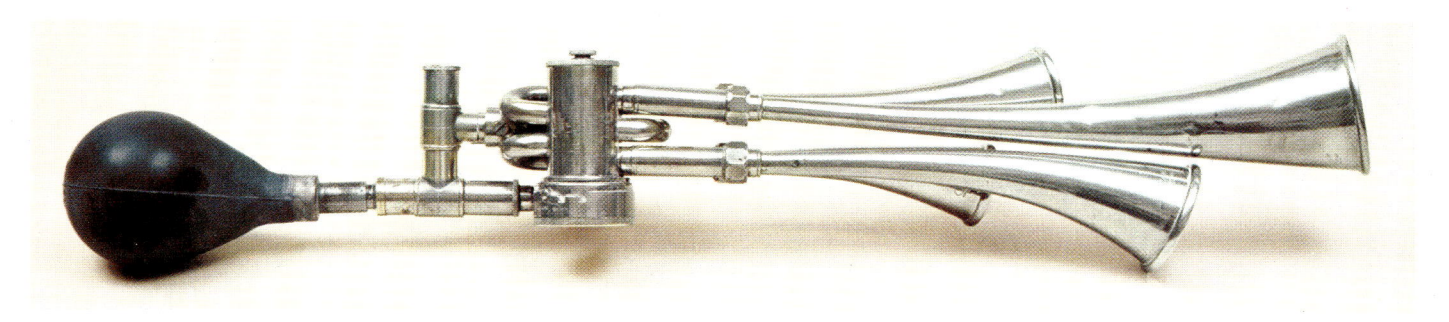

One of the most elaborate and expensive bulb horns was the Testaphone, made in France after World War I. When the bulb was squeezed, it played four notes in preprogramed mechanical progression. One popular tune was the opening bars of "The Marseillaise."

these plates before they cut up a car and keep them in the proverbial cigar box—possibly to make them available to sheriffs tracking down stolen cars. Nowadays an old cigar box is a collector's item itself. On one or two occasions I have been lucky enough to acquire in one swoop both a box and a cache of serial plates from an earlier generation of auto wrecking.

Secondary hallmarks of the early cars were certain small parts, such as the hubcap. It almost always carried the name of the car, and sometimes added a distinctive design: Packard's was a red hexagon; Pierce-Arrow's had an arrow. Early hubcaps were made of brass and not only make fine collector pieces but also can be useful—they often serve as attractive and unusual paperweights. The later aluminum caps are almost as good for this purpose. But the big, easily dented pie-plate shapes of the 1930s are much less desirable.

Nowadays hubcaps have become strictly utilitarian, and are concealed by wheel covers that have a diameter just less than that of the inside of the tire. These covers too may command high prices; a wheel cover from a 1956 Lincoln Continental Mark II, for example, which cost $56 when it was brand new, was still worth almost as much as that 20 years later. And a set of wheel covers for a late-model Rolls-Royce can cost up to $300.

Years ago the best place to find old hubcaps was the junk box of a corner garage, but I once picked up an early brass-and-aluminum beauty from the ledge of an

New Jersey's 1912 license plates had space for the car's serial number. New York's 1912 plates can be dated by their color: white on red.

These enamel badges of the 1920s identified members of the American Automobile Association and the National Motorists Association.

old barn within the New York city limits. I had gone to this building, a relic from the days when the place was a working farm, to track down a lead about an old car that was supposed to be on the premises. There was no car, only a hubcap. It was from a 1907 Thomas Flyer, and the price was right: 25 cents. Such hubcaps now fetch from $10 to $40 depending on age, rarity and condition.

Like hubcaps, radiator caps are essential parts of cars and have undergone a series of transformations. Originally they were unremarkable seals for the coolant, with nothing but shape to identify them: the one for the Model T Ford, for example, has four little nubs to make it easier to turn. But one type that is easy to match to the car it fitted is the Moto-Meter—a thermometer-equipped cap that indicated engine temperature in the days before dashboard warning signals. Each one bore a miniature of the name plate of the car it belonged to.

The utilitarian stopper soon blossomed with ornamental designs. Some, made for automobiles long out of production, are identifiable only by an expert. But others—the Pontiac Indian chief, the Mercedes three-pointed star—are known to almost everyone. Most famous of all is the Rolls-Royce Spirit of Ecstasy, or, as it is more commonly known, the Flying Lady. Early examples signed by the designer, Charles Sykes, are of great value. I have seen them go at flea markets for $100.

Such standardized identification did not satisfy some early motoring enthusiasts, who wanted personalized marks on their cars and ordered radiator caps custom-made in fancy shops like Nil Melior's in New York City. It was fashionable, if you could afford it, to proclaim a

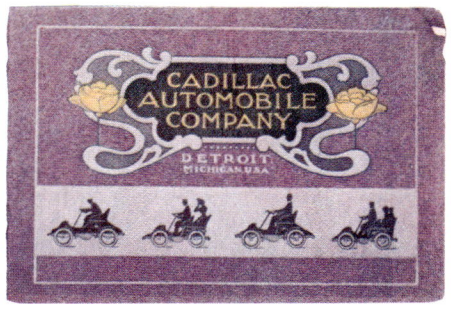

The 1939 Buick catalogue featured technical-looking diagrams of such items as the hood insignia and clock; the 1929 Chrysler cata-logue played up the classy 65 and 75 models. The first Cadillac catalogue, issued before the car was built, showed it in silhouette.

hobby or interest by means of your radiator cap, and people ordered cast-metal figurines of dogs, horses, eagles, storks and warrior heads. Probably the most unusual special-order radiator-cap ornaments are those of crystal in a number of styles by René Lalique, the renowned French glassmaker.

A famous example of an exotic radiator cap was the cobra used by film idol Rudolph Valentino on his Isotta-Fraschini. After Valentino's death, this cobra cap continued to be made in small quantities, and several examples of the original design still exist, including the one on the Isotta that was being delivered to him at the time of his death. Meanwhile, the Isotta company made the cobra motif available as an option on all its cars—so a cobra cap is not as special as it might at first seem to be.

In the 1930s, when the radiator began to be covered by grille and hood, the cap once again became a plain stopper. But many designs remained as hood ornaments, and they too are collectors' items—chief among them the Rolls Royce Flying Lady and the Lalique crystal ornaments, which are still being made. A modern Lalique is worth about $100; the old ones even more. Color is the clue to the difference between them: the modern ornaments are clear white, while their predecessors are tinged with purple.

Only somewhat less subtle than Lalique crystal as status symbols were club badges. They were particularly popular with the British, many of whom installed between the headlamps "badge bars" capable of holding as many as half a dozen club emblems. Many of these motoring clubs were as difficult to get into as the social

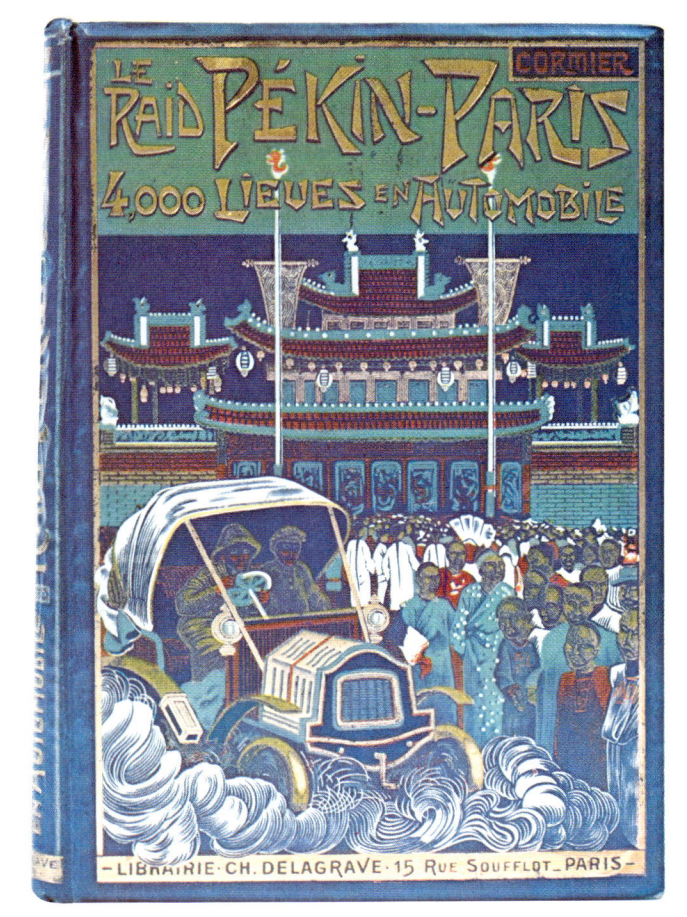

A valuable automobile book is "Le Raid Pekin-Paris," which told of a 1907 China-to-France race. The car shown is a De Dion-Bouton.

108 / AUTOMOBILIA

Souvenirs to Carry

Early motoring enthusiasts often carried tokens of their automotive interests on their persons, or displayed them on desks or bookcases. Some of these souvenirs served a practical purpose, such as holding cigarettes or liquor; others decorated the special costumes that were designed to ward off the rigors of riding in open vehicles. Like the early cars themselves, which were finely crafted objects, many of the mementos were exquisite examples of the jeweler's art.

Motoring pins from about 1900 were often bejeweled, like the lower of these two, which has a pearl steering wheel.

A 1920s lapel pin, worn by salesmen for the custom-made Belgian Minerva, is as rare and elegant as the car itself.

A silver cigarette case depicts in cloisonné enamel a 1902 racing car traveling at full speed. In the days before pit stops, the mechanic rode along as a working passenger.

An amber glass whiskey flask archly disguises its contents as cylinder oil.

register. But their badges, although issued to members only, now and then turn up at flea markets and rummage sales. One of the finest collections of motoring-club badges, incidentally, is displayed on the walls of a New York restaurant, Le Chanteclair, whose part owner was once a noted French racing-car driver.

At the other end of the status ladder from badges and custom-made radiator ornaments—but equally collectible—is a plebeian identification: the license plate. Licensing was introduced around the turn of the century. I know from family experience that New York City required licenses as early as 1901. In a clumsy attempt to help a run-over pedestrian to identify the driver who had just hit him, the law stipulated that the owner's initials be displayed on the back of the car in letters 3 to 4 inches high. I remember this because my father was arrested for driving his Locomobile Steamer without the initials. He took the case to court, where he won, the judge ruling the law unconstitutional because it was discriminatory: it applied only to pleasure cars.

In 1902 New York state assigned numbers to cars and furnished each owner with a small metal disk that was supposed to be mounted on the dashboard. At the same time the owner, at his own expense, went to his harness maker and had a leather license plate made up with aluminum numbers like the numbers that mark houses. This hung from the car's back axle by small straps. When several states began to issue standardized license plates, around 1909, New York's were made of porcelainized steel. They are very durable and occasionally a perfect one can be dug up from underground. The first of these plates were undated and were valid permanently; around 1910, annual plates came into use. Porcelainized steel plates in good condition are very desirable; I have seen a perfect pair at a flea market priced at $100. Chipped ones command around $10 or $15.

For beginning collectors, the Bicentennial celebrations of 1976 provide a once-in-a-lifetime opportunity to build up a collection of interesting plates at little expense. Many states included a special notation on plates for that year. I have seen them advertised in unused condition for as little as a couple of dollars each. It would be quite an undertaking to get a complete set, but the result would be impressive.

Even greater and more varied than the categories of automobilia fastened to cars are those that are not. These include such items as road signs and garage signs, as well as all kinds of automobile art, from catalogue covers and advertisements to books and paintings, paperweights, souvenir mugs, fine china and jewelry.

Not long ago, I was lucky enough to find several very fine road signs *(page 110)* of porcelainized steel that had been put up at the junctions of country roads on the north shore of Long Island by the Long Island Automobile Club, in the days before sign posting became a government function.

Another sought-after type of sign is the advertisement that used to be posted over the door of the local repair shop, promoting service for a particular make of car or a brand of batteries or tires—such nostalgia-evoking names as Diamond, G & J and Para, as well as the more familiar Firestone, Goodrich and Goodyear. Most of these vintage garage signs were made of painted or lithographed steel, which rusts fairly easily, and they are hard to find in good condition.

Signs are a kind of folk art, but more sophisticated drawings and paintings related to automobiles make up an important part of automobilia collectibles. Generally they are representational—the cars look like cars. They were done by leading artists and illustrators of the times, who were commissioned to produce advertisements and magazine covers on the subject.

Because most of these works were made simply for commercial use in reproduction, few originals survive. One that I have shows a 1905 Mercedes with a view of the old Madison Square Garden in the background, done for the cover of a January 21, 1905, auto-show issue of *Collier's (page 111)*. The artist is J. C. Leyendecker, the popular turn-of-the-century illustrator who created the Arrow Collar Man. The Mercedes cover is a special prize because the car is unusual. Although a German make, it was assembled in the United States from some imported parts and some parts manufactured at a Mercedes plant in Long Island City, New York.

While original automobile art like the Leyendecker painting may be hard to find, reproductions are not. Some were made to be sold as prints for framing, and thus were produced in relatively limited numbers, but most appeared in magazines, of which hundreds of thousands or even millions of copies were printed.

The most desirable and expensive automobile art are the prints intended for framing made before World War I, particularly those produced between 1904 and 1913 by Edouard Montaut in Paris. Most are impressionistic racing scenes, which Montaut sketched at the event and then turned into lithographs in his studio. His studio came to include a dozen or so assistants—one of whom, a man who simply signed his name Gamy, later produced lithographs on his own in the same style as Montaut—plus a group of young women who colored each print by hand. The colors of Montaut's prints were delightful, but they faded badly when exposed to daylight for any length of time. New, they could be purchased for $10 or $15; three quarters of a century later a Montaut in good condition fetched $200 or $300.

During a second historical period, between the two World Wars, the best-known automotive artist was F. Gordon Crosby, whose paintings appeared in the British

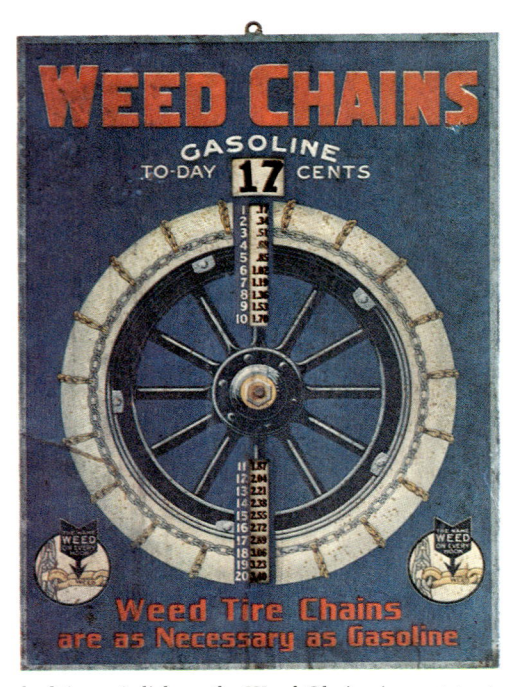

The garage sign above has a value beyond its age—it dates from 1916—because it memorializes a famous racing-car driver who lent his name to a brand of tires. A disk on the Weed Chain sign rotates to display gasoline prices; its highest setting is 39 cents a gallon.

magazine *Autocar.* From time to time, the magazine published sets of Crosby reproductions in miniature size, and some can still be found, particularly in England. He too portrayed racing events, but his pictures are full of detail and motion, quite unlike Montaut's.

After World War II, the explosion of interest in automobiles led to a third flowering of automotive art. The two great artists of this period were Peter Helck and Leslie Saalburg, both Americans. Saalburg began his work in the '20s, painting Lincoln advertisements, but they are unsigned and can be identified only by his style. During the 1950s he produced fine covers for *Esquire* that usually depicted impeccably dressed people in finely detailed compositions of such events as auto shows. He also frequently did automotive illustrations for *The Lamp,* the magazine published by the Exxon Corporation and its predecessor companies. Peter Helck, too, worked for *Esquire,* and his series of eight automobile paintings for that magazine, all but one of them on racing, are in my opinion unusually fine. Helck was enormously prolific—at 83 he still had a three-year backlog of commissions—and few collectors own a complete set of his prints, advertisements and other creations, among them two books, *Great Auto Races* and *The Checkered Flag.* Recently at a flea market I found an advertisement signed by Helck, one I had never seen. I grabbed it. When going through stacks of old magazines, watch for any advertisement signed simply H, the form Helck frequently used to identify his work.

In the days before highway departments put up road signs, automobile clubs often provided them. This porcelain-on-steel sign told motorists which way to turn but not how far they had to go.

Automobile advertisements from old magazines are, in fact, one of the easiest kinds of automobilia to assemble. They are readily available, inexpensive—especially if you thumb through stacks at garage sales and flea markets—and they take up very little space. They also provide interesting and valuable information about old cars at a far cheaper price than the principal source of such data, the voluminous and varied literature concerned with automobiles.

Many automotive books are personal accounts of memorable trips, or biographies. I have more than 70 devoted to Henry Ford or his cars, and about 10 new ones appear each year. But of more direct interest to

AUTOMOBILIA / 111

For a 1905 automobile-show issue, Collier's magazine commissioned this cover painting by J. C. Leyendecker of a Mercedes; in the background is New York's old Madison Square Garden.

Original automobile art, such as this 1908 portrait by Warren B. Davis, is scarce.

A specialist in prints of automobile races, the French artist Edouard Montaut produced this scene of driver Léon Duray tearing along in his Lorraine-Dietrich in the Gordon Bennett elimination race, held in the French province of Auvergne in 1905.

112 / AUTOMOBILIA

Postcards that include vintage trucks and automobiles often offer unwitting glimpses of social history. At left is a prize-winning WCTU float on an unidentifiable 1916 truck body, together with the cup it won (insert) in a parade. At right, above, is a tourist bus in Yosemite Park, and below is a Pope Hartford bus fitted out as a police van by the Hartford, Connecticut, police department.

collectors are books, pamphlets and magazines that contain detailed and technical information about old cars.

Perhaps the most sought-after type of automobile literature is the car catalogue. It was given away free at automobile shows, was seldom kept beyond its year of publication and consequently became quite rare in just a few years' time. Prices of considerably more than $100 have been asked for a single catalogue from as recent a period as the 1930s.

Several other pieces of similarly valuable literature are the instruction books and service manuals issued for cars, and salesmen's data books and showroom catalogues. Both the instruction book and the service manual contain technical data, the former for the car owner, the latter for the garage mechanic. The salesmen's data books, many of them pocket size, contain answers to all the questions likely to be asked by prospective customers. The showroom catalogue, a voluminous affair, contains information on all the optional trim and paint choices available to the customer and often includes actual swatches of paint colors and fabrics. Showroom catalogues are very rare; even a modern one is hard to acquire. One way to get them is to ask a friendly dealer to save them for you when the model year ends.

Supplementing the catalogues and manuals issued by car makers are handbooks put out every year by associations of automobile manufacturers. The handbooks assemble in single volumes data on many makes of cars. The first, called *Hand Book of Gasoline Automobiles*, was published in 1904 by the Association of Licensed Automobile Manufacturers. You could get it then by sending in a six-cent stamp, but during the 1970s a $100 bill would have failed to move one. The same organization put out the book each year through 1911. In 1912 and 1913, it was issued under the same name by the Automobile Board of Trade in the United States, and then it was carried on through 1929 as the *Hand Book of Automobiles* by the National Automobile Chamber of Commerce. The least expensive handbook from this period you are likely to find costs at least $35 today.

An even rarer and more complete handbook is the *MoToR Directory of Motor Cars*, put out by *MoToR* magazine in the early years of the automobile industry. It contained statistics on every automobile the editors could find out about. These directories are now worth about $100 when one turns up, which is not very often.

Specialized periodicals such as *MoToR* are themselves collectibles. An early American magazine, *Motocycle*, was published in October 1895 but folded soon afterward. The first with any longevity was *The Horseless Age*, which began publication on November 1, 1895, and continued until 1918. *MoToR* appeared around the turn of the century, along with *The Automobile* (later called *Automotive Industries*), *Cycle and Automobile Trade Journal*, *Automobile Topics*, *Motor Age* and *Motor World*.

One day after the first issue of *The Horseless Age* appeared, the British magazine *Autocar* came out in London; it was joined in 1903 by *The Motor*. In France in the years before the First World War there were at least three magazines—*Omnia*, *La France Automobile* and

In 1904 Royal Doulton produced in limited quantities a set of dinnerware that found humor in such predicaments as breakdowns and pairs of hitchhikers. A complete set of this china is now almost unobtainable, and the price for a single pitcher is likely to be $100.

The same lady, posed in the same car, graces two pieces of inexpensive pottery that might fetch $10 as automobilia. At left, she appears on a calendar plate for 1909, given away as an advertisement by an Iowa merchant; at right, she decorates an earthenware mug.

114/AUTOMOBILIA

A souvenir pennant commemorates a famous auto race held annually between 1904 and 1916. One of the prime sporting events of the year, the Vanderbilt Cup attracted huge crowds; the 1906 race on Long Island drew two million, the largest audience in sports history.

This sterling-silver-and-staghorn trophy was presented in 1904 to the winner of a 6,293-foot race up Mt. Washington in New Hampshire.

La Vie Automobile—and in Germany there was *Der Motorwagen*, first published in 1898.

To round out my own collection of automobilia I have accumulated a catchall of miscellaneous items. There are programs from the Vanderbilt Cup Races, which were held—usually on Long Island—from 1904 to 1916, the golden age of auto racing. And I have a fascinating array of old photographs in which automobiles appear, either as the subject or in the background. Every flea market seems to have a few examples of these, and so far the prices have remained moderate; they can usually be bought for less than five dollars. Postcards that show cars are also part of my collection; these are becoming harder to find because they are so popular.

Other curiosities I have picked up in my collecting career are glass paperweights with photographs of cars embedded in them; bronze paperweights given away as advertisements by such firms as Packard, Chalmers and DeDion; letter openers and knives with pictures of cars on their handles; shaving mugs and beer mugs decorated with likenesses of cars; souvenir plates and even a few pieces of fine Royal Doulton china with motoring scenes depicted on them. I also have a collection of jewelry that uses cars as ornaments—ladies' pins, gentlemen's stickpins and many lapel pins worn by salesmen in automobile showrooms. A salesman's lapel pin is a relatively common article, but some of them are highly desirable. The three-pointed star pin worn by Mercedes-Benz salesmen is particularly hard to come by, although I suppose that if you drop by the local Mercedes dealer, order the new model and then ask the salesman for his pin, he could hardly refuse you.

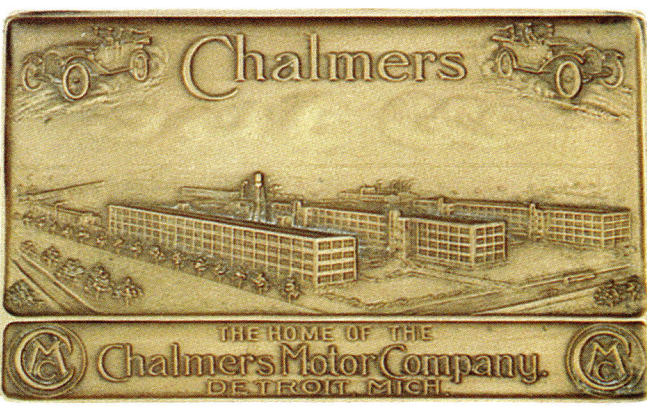

In 1914 Packard put its familiar slogan and the outline of its grille on a paperweight (top), while Chalmers in the same year advertised its plant; both paperweights are bronze.

Reproductions of older versions of these lapel pins have been around for years, and turn up so often at flea markets and thrift shops that you have to look carefully to tell whether the one you have is four or 40 years old. There is so much interest in old cars today that almost every item considered automobilia is being remanufactured. Usually these replicas look suspiciously new—but this is not an infallible clue. I have seen reproductions of garage signs that have been artificially aged, right down to the rust. Often the only way to spot a copy is to compare it with an original point by point—a task aided, fortunately, by the wide availability of descriptions, pictures and authentic artifacts of automobilia.

For related material, see the article on Cars in a separate volume of this encyclopedia.

MUSEUMS
Bellm's Cars & Music of Yesterday
Sarasota, Florida 33580

Briggs Cunningham Automotive Museum
Costa Mesa, California 92626

Frederick C. Crawford Auto-Aviation Museum
Cleveland, Ohio 44106

Harrah's Automobile Collection
Reno, Nevada 89504

Long Island Automotive Museum
Southampton, New York 11968

Museum of Transportation
Brookline, Massachusetts 02146

Swigart Museum
Huntingdon, Pennsylvania 11652

COLLECTORS ORGANIZATIONS
Antique Automobile Club of America
501 West Governor Road
Hershey, Pennsylvania 17033

Hubcap Collector's Club
c/o Dennis Kuhn
Box 54
Buckley, Michigan 49620

Michigan License Plate Collectors Association
601 Duchess Road
Milford, Michigan 48042

Veteran Motor Car Club of America
105 Elm Street
Andover, Massachusetts 01810

PERIODICALS
Automobile Quarterly, Automobile Quarterly, Inc., Kutztown, Pennsylvania 19530

Car Classics, Car Classics Publishing Co., Chatsworth, California 91311

Cars and Parts, George Slankard, Sesser, Illinois 62884

Old Cars, Chester L. Krause, Iola, Wisconsin 54945

BOOKS
Dyke, A. L., *Dyke's Automobile and Gasoline Engine Encyclopedia.* Goodheart-Willcox, Inc., 1943.

Homans, James E., *Self-Propelled Vehicles.* Theo. Audel & Co., 1902.

Page, Victor:
The Modern Gasoline Automobile. Norman W. Henley, 1912.
Questions and Answers Relating to Automobile Design. Norman W. Henley, 1916.

Girl Skipping Rope was regarded by workers who made it as one of their more difficult assignments, requiring an intricate, multipiece casting. It is the official symbol of the collectors society, the Mechanical Bank Collectors of America. The bank was designed and patented by J. H. Bowen of Philadelphia in 1890, and was made by the J & E Stevens Manufacturing Company of Cromwell, Connecticut.

Banks
Making a Game of Moneysaving

Many years ago, on a visit to an antique dealer's in search of china, my mother was shown a small mechanical bank in the shape of the infamous old Tammany Hall leader, Boss Tweed. It had an interesting action. You put a coin in Tweed's hand, and he immediately stuffed it in his pocket while nodding his head to say "thank you." As I was in the business of manufacturing safes, the dealer and my mother thought I would enjoy it, and she bought it for me.

The next Christmas I went shopping for presents at the same dealer's and he had another mechanical bank I thought amusing. I bought it. From then on, whenever I came across a bank that had an interesting action I picked it up. One day I realized I had about 35 banks. Without trying to, I had become a collector.

The first mass-produced American toy banks were "still" banks—banks with no mechanical action. One of

---

Edwin H. Mosler comes by an interest in banks naturally, for he is the retired head of the safe and vault manufacturing company that bears his name. He has been collecting banks for 25 years.

---

the earliest was a penny bank made to accommodate the first large copper coin minted in 1793 by the new government. Mechanical banks appeared during the 1860s; a patent for a mechanical bank called Hall's Excelsior was filed in 1869.

The heyday of production was the period between 1860 and 1935; some 400 distinct types were made and for each there were usually many variations. When one manufacturer produced a popular bank, his competitors were likely to copy it—with just enough alterations to skirt any possible suit for patent infringement. I suppose I now have about 1,500 banks in my collection but I still do not own examples of 24 basic types. I know where 22 of them are, but it will take some time to gather them up since their owners are also collectors and are not anxious to trade or sell.

Mechanical banks were toys intended to encourage children to save their pennies by making the process fun. In some the mechanical action rewarded the child with a piece of candy. But essentially the banks were simply designed to amuse children with the intricacy of

The Clown and Globe bank, which dates from around 1890, was produced in great quantity and is relatively easy to find. When activated, the clown performs a handstand.

117

118 / BANKS

The lady Columbine, a stock pantomime character, dances around a clown and her partner, Harlequin, on this 1906 bank.

In this Mikado bank a Japanese figure moves the coin between cymbals, as in a shell game, and always wins for the bank.

Portraying a Biblical tale, the great whale on this 1890 pedestal bank coughs up a happy Jonah on receipt of a coin.

The teller on this rare Freedman's bank of the post-Civil War era thumbs his nose while he takes the money.

As the ticket man stands by the coin slot, the five animals on this 1890s Merry-Go-Round bank journey in an endless circle.

In this Little Red Riding Hood bank, Grandma's mask falls away when the coin drops in, revealing the wicked wolf.

The craze for roller-skating contests inspired this rare turn-of-the-century bank on which a girl wins the prize wreath.

This bank shows the infamous William Tweed, boss of Tammany Hall, the political club that ruled New York City in the 19th Century and milked millions from public funds. The bank is operated by handing Tweed a coin. He then pockets it while nodding his thanks.

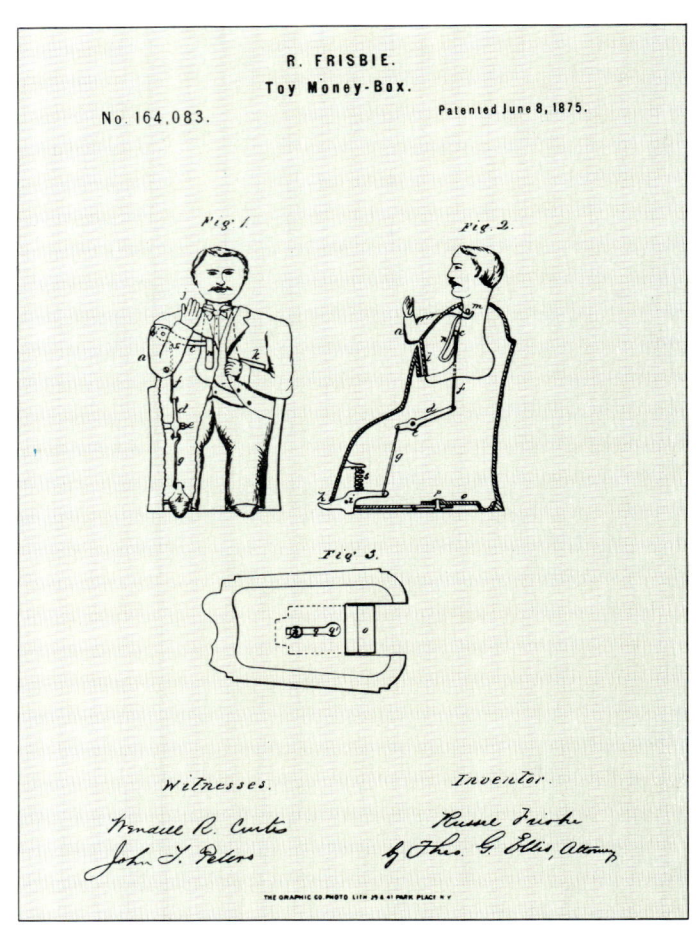

A clue to the age of the Tammany Bank, invented by Russel Frisbie, is provided by patent drawings issued in 1875. Accompanied by an explanation of the mechanism, they were meant to prevent copying, a common practice in the freebooting days of the late 19th Century.

their mechanical actions, which could be started by depositing a coin or depressing a lever.

Mechanical banks made of cast iron became popular shortly after the end of the Civil War, when several Northern foundries started producing them as a profitable side line to their regular business of casting such items as stovepipes, plumbing pipes and tools. The J & E Stevens Company of Cromwell, Connecticut, was one of the most prominent. Manufacturers competed to see how complex they could make their banks' operation. One of my favorites shows William Tell and his son *(opposite)*. When you put in a coin, William Tell shoots the coin at the apple on the boy's head and knocks the apple off. The coin drops into the bank behind the son, who then raises his hand to protect himself.

To perform stunts like this, mechanical banks relied on various combinations of levers, springs, wheels and other moving parts. In some the weight of the coin plays an essential role by moving a lever from one position to another, causing a wheel to rotate, and that in turn activates another part. Naturally, the more intricate the outer action of the bank, the more ingenious the inner mechanism. A particularly complex contraption operates another favorite of mine, a hunter who actually brings down a bird *(page 123)*. The mechanical action sends the bird flying—it is attached to a string. The hunter turns and fires, and the bird drops.

Some banks tell little stories from American history. Even before the trust-busting days of Teddy Roosevelt there was a bank that showed a workingman hitting "big business" with a sledge hammer, whereupon the coin dropped into a breadbasket labeled "Honest Labor." And one of the rarest mechanical banks, called the Freedman's bank *(page 119)*, reflects the racism of the 19th Century. In it a black bank teller sits behind a cashier's desk. When a coin is placed on the desk, the teller grasps it with his left hand and thumbs his nose with his right. Obviously the bank was intended to make an antiblack comment on the behavior of freed slaves after the Civil War. This bank was made by Jerome

Three stages in the manufacture of a cast-iron bank are illustrated above for the William Tell bank, in which the legendary archer shoots an apple off his son's head when a penny is dropped into the castle. In the first step a master pattern is carved of wood (bottom), which is used to make a reverse mold of the pattern in sand. The mold is used to cast a second pattern of brass (top), and from this brass pattern a second mold is made of sand or plaster of paris. The second mold is used in casting the finished product in iron (center).

Secor of Bridgeport, Connecticut, and, as far as I know, only five exist. Ethnic bigotry is discernible in many old banks. I have several that poke fun at the Irish and Chinese immigrants brought in to provide cheap labor during the building of the railroads. One depicts a lazy-looking Chinese laborer playing cards lying down *(page 125)*. Another has Paddy, the traditional Irish comic figure, sitting with a pig *(page 125)*.

But the kinds of mechanical banks I enjoy most have an interesting action as well as historical significance. The sophistication of the mechanism is important. For example, one shows a young girl skipping rope *(page 116)*. It would be enough, perhaps, just to have her jump up and down. She does that, but at each jump she also turns her head to the side and steps over the rope one leg at a time, just the way a little girl would.

Rope-skipping is only one of many complex acts put on by these mechanical toys. When a coin is placed in the Clown and Harlequin bank *(page 118)*, Harlequin's partner, Columbine, does a twirling dance in a slot that runs partway around a small stage. The confidence man's old shell game is played by a bank called the Mikado—it portrays a Japanese who uses two cymbals in place of shells to hide the coin. When the coin is put down, the Mikado's arms move the cymbals over it. First you see the coin under one cymbal, then under the other—and then it disappears inside the bank. Another bank has a racecourse with two horses on a circular track *(page 123)*. The deposit of a coin sets the horses running, and either horse can win because the spring that sets them off flicks both horses simultaneously.

In the days when mechanical banks were in their prime, moral uplift was an important theme and so some banks had Biblical motifs. On one the coin gets a whale to spit up Jonah *(page 118)*. Political subjects were also popular. When Germany's Chancellor Bismarck put a tariff on American pork, an American manufacturer brought out a bank that had the unpopular Bismarck popping up out of the body of a pig *(page 125)*.

During World War I, when the production of cast

122 / BANKS

On the Darktown Battery bank, the pitcher throws a penny at the batter, who swings but has not made a hit in 111 years. The catcher then drops the coin into a slot in his chest. Racist and ethnic prejudices often crept into the characterization of such figures.

Called the Calamity bank, this portrayal of an unsuccessful play in a football game is filled with action. When the coin is dropped, the ball carrier turns from the position at left and leans forward to run upfield. But the tacklers also turn—and stop the runner for no gain.

BANKS / 123

Unlike most mechanical banks, in which the action is unvaryingly repeated, this 1871 race-track bank has two horses that are started off by the unpredictable flicking motion of a spring. In the ensuing dash around the track, either horse may win.

The Fowler bank's lifelike imitation of a hunting scene includes a bird that "flies" out on a string when a coin is inserted. The bird is realistically brought down by the hunter with a gun that fires caps.

When a coin is put into this 1879 bank, the bowler releases the ball, which knocks down the pins and rings a bell. Because of its movable ball and 10 small pins it is hard to find this bank intact.

124 / BANKS

A modern version of an old idea is the Bicentennial Betsy Ross bank. When a lever is pressed, Betsy turns to her sewing basket.

Much of the craftsmanship commonplace in 19th Century banks is lacking in this modern bank, which capitalizes on the 1973 tennis match between Bobby Riggs and Billie Jean King. The figures are less finely detailed, the casting less smooth and the joints less carefully fitted.

iron for civilian use was severely limited, manufacturers began to use tin, wood and other materials for banks. Now, of course, many banks are made of plastic. Most serious collectors reject plastic banks, having rather arbitrarily agreed among themselves that mechanical banks are collectible only if they were made before 1935. For myself, I don't agree. My collection includes, for example, a green plastic mechanical bank in the shape of Big Bird, a character in TV's *Sesame Street,* and a cast-iron bank of the '70s showing Uncle Sam arguing with an Arab over oil. I also have a cast-iron bank based on the much-publicized tennis match between Bobby Riggs and Billie Jean King in 1973 *(above, right)*. If a new mechanical bank were to be made tomorrow morning, I would want a model for my collection by afternoon.

Although still banks interest me, too, and an almost unlimited number of these banks are available from all historical periods, I have not tried to collect them with the same passion or interest. From time to time, I have picked up unusual still banks mostly to use as lagniappe in trading with other collectors who have mechanical banks I want. Trading between experienced collectors can sometimes become extremely sharp, and still banks, I have discovered, make excellent trading counters for reaching a mutually agreeable exchange.

When I first started, I collected anything that appealed to me. I still do. But I always try for mint

This pineapple-head bank, issued to mark the entry of Hawaii into the Union as the 50th state in 1959, uses a mechanism common to many banks. It is activated by a lever in the back when a coin is placed in its hand. The coin is brought to the mouth and swallowed.

BANKS / 125

The only President known to be immortalized in a cast-iron mechanical bank is Theodore Roosevelt. In this bank, a bear's head appears at the top of the tree when Teddy fires a penny into the trunk.

Typical of mechanical banks that, a century ago, ridiculed minorities are these, in which an obsequious black tips his hat, a shanty Irishman cuddles his pig, and an indolent Chinese cardplayer with four aces in his hand smiles inscrutably. All three are from the 1880s.

The Bismarck bank pokes none-too-sly fun at the German Chancellor, who put an import restriction on American pork products. In this retaliatory design Bismarck's head pops out of the body of a pig when a coin is put into the slot and the pig's tail is pushed down.

126 / BANKS

Lighter and simpler than cast-iron banks, these German banks from the 1920s and 1930s are lithographed tin. The figures' jaws drop when a coin is inserted. From the left, they are the British Lion, a bulldog, a teddy bear, an African native and film star Harold Lloyd.

A deposit in this 19th Century German bank brings a quick dividend: a piece of candy.

The Ding Dong Bell bank of the 1880s provides a 20-second show. When a coin is inserted, one boy rings a bell. Another, on the fence, waves his hat while a third pulls a cat from a well.

An enduring favorite, the Trick Dog bank has been reproduced in a number of variations through the years. It is activated by a lever when a penny is put into the dog's mouth. The dog then executes a leap through the clown's hoop and deposits the coin in the barrel. At upper right is a modern version of this complicated circus act, in plastic; the other four examples are older. The original model (top row, center) was introduced by the Hubley Manufacturing Company in 1888; the other three are 19th Century imitations of it.

condition. A bank that has been extensively restored has lost much of its value even if great care has been exercised. Badly restored banks give themselves away by looking freshly painted or having crudely joined parts. Whenever I have to have a bank restored, I cannibalize parts from other banks made during the same period and I have the work done by a craftsman whose passion for authenticity matches my own.

Although I value my collection for its condition, I do not worry about its market value. That's for investors, not collectors. Sometimes, I must admit, I am shocked to find out how high prices have gone in recent years. A bank that once sold for $4,500 was bid up to $14,000 in one sale—and the last price tends to become the floor for the next time around. That Tammany bank my mother bought in fun in 1952 was selling 25 years later for $130 in good condition. That's expensive for a joke.

Because of the banks' monetary value, some collectors keep theirs under lock and key. But I like to show mine to other collectors, so I display them in my office, which is protected with a burglar alarm. Included in the display is a considerable assemblage of related materials—patent models, advertising brochures and the original molds from which the banks were made. I even have a few examples of fake banks. These are usually mechanical toys to which coin slots were later added. Then the toys were passed off as true mechanical banks.

Despite its breadth, my collection is simply a source of pleasure to me, not a scholarly aggregation of artifacts. In fact, I keep a privately published book in my office for visiting collectors to read: *What I Know about Collecting Mechanical Banks*. Its pages are entirely blank. But my shelves are filled with things I love.

For related material, see the article on Toys in a separate volume of this encyclopedia.

MUSEUMS
The Museum of the City of New York
New York, New York 10029

Perelman Antique Toy Museum
Philadelphia, Pennsylvania 19106

Seaman's Bank for Savings
New York, New York 10005

BOOKS
Hertz, Louis H., *Mechanical Toy Banks.* Mark Haber, 1947.

McCumber, Robert L., *Toy Bank Reproductions and Fakes.* Published by the author, 1971.

Meyer, John D., and Larry Freeman, *Old Penny Banks: Mechanicals, Stills.* Century House, Inc., 1960.

Warman, Edwin G., *Mechanicals and Stills Price Guide.* E. G. Warman Publishing, Inc., 1975.

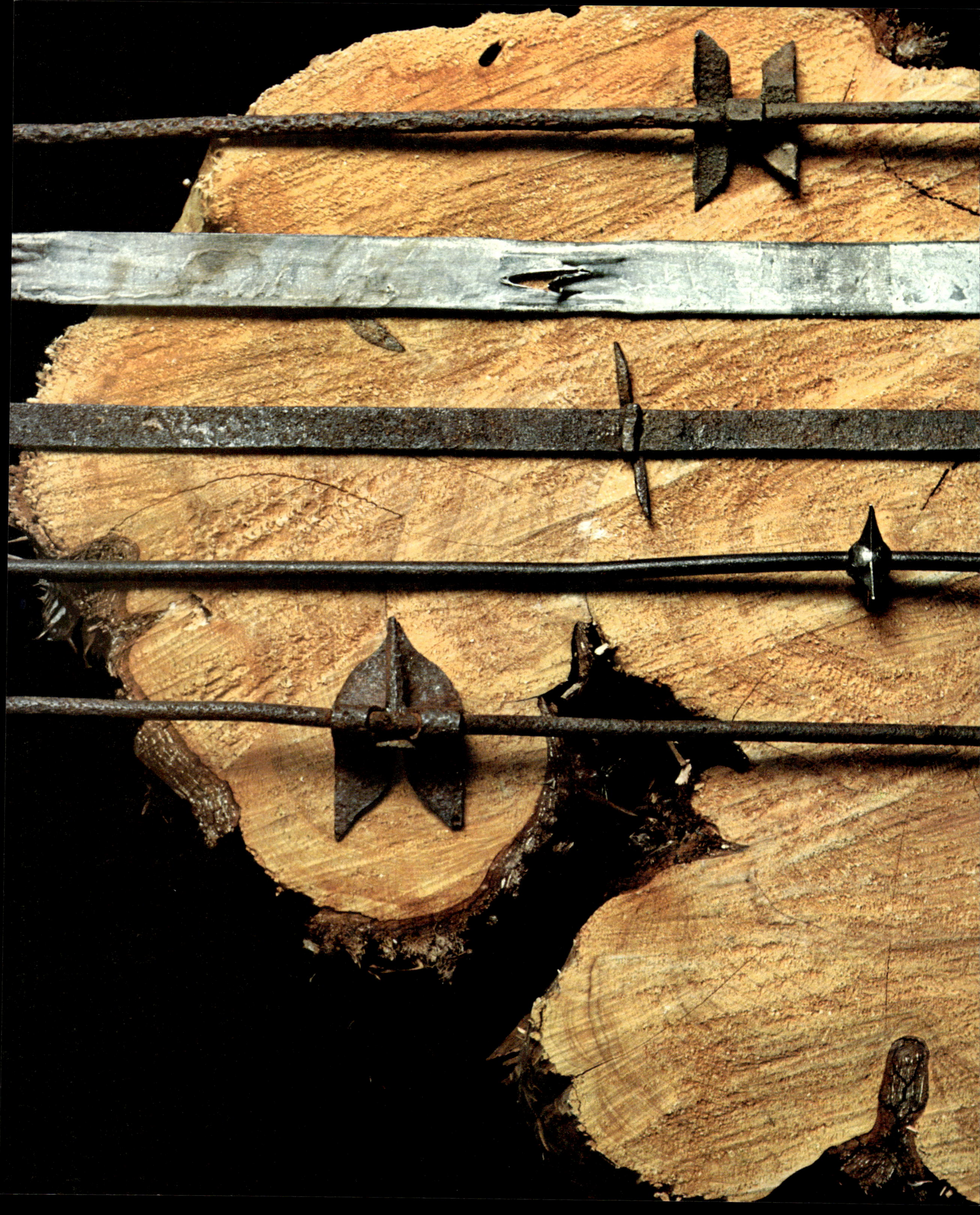

Barbed Wire
Trophy of Westward Expansion

Many factors influenced the settling of the Western United States, but few caused as much wrangling as the introduction of barbed wire. The first confrontations were between cattlemen and farmers. The former, needing access for their herds to publicly owned unoccupied grazing land, resisted the very idea of fences. The latter, wanting to protect their fields from wandering cattle, looked upon fences as a necessity and quickly adopted barbed wire because it was quicker and cheaper to install than fences of stone and wood. Later, the railroads

C. W. "Smokey" Doyle, a Texan who became interested in barbed wire while studying his region's history, has been collecting since 1968. He now owns more than 400 kinds and is still going strong.

entered the controversy. They strung barbed wire along their rights-of-way to protect trains from herds of cattle and buffalo. Some historians even suggest that the railroads built fences to seal off the famous cattle trails and force cattlemen to ship their animals to market by train. Considering the importance of barbed wire to the history of the West, it is little wonder that some 100,000 people find wire collecting a fascinating avocation.

Though barbed wire's widespread use was inevitable, it took salesmanship to get the newfangled idea accepted. One enterprising wire salesman, John Warne Gates, nicknamed "Bet-a-Million" Gates, has gone down in Western lore as a supersalesman who made money twice on one grand demonstration. Gates announced that he was staging a rodeo in San Antonio with a special added attraction: a barbed-wire corral he guaranteed would hold overnight the orneriest cattle anyone could find. This was an invitation that grizzled old ranchers could not turn down. About 75 steers, chosen for their mean dispositions, were placed in the corral and bets were placed on the outcome. Gates cheerfully took all bets against his fence and even went so far as to hire riders to

The wires at left—some oddly named—are among the most sought after. From the top are: Scutt's Butterfly Clip; Woodcock, a die-cut barb; Upham's Smashed Loop; Reynolds, with a nonrusting zinc barb; and the Harsha, with a nail forced through for an extra point.

Desirable, but not the costliest, rarities are these wires, worth around $50 each in the late 1970s. At the top is Burrows Joined Diamonds; in the center, a relatively rare two-holed version of Drilled Plate (in a commoner version the plate has one hole); at bottom, a steel half-round rod, pierced with a barb.

Four wires that are inexpensive and not hard for a beginning collector to find are, from top to bottom, Brinkerhoff Ribbon Wire; Daniel C. Stover Two-Line Wire; Scutt's Single Clip; and Hodge's Spur Rowel, which has a revolving barb.

129

The Great Barb Patent Rush

During the last three decades of the 19th Century the U.S. Patent Office was inundated by applications from inventors rushing to cash in on the barbed-wire boom. More than 700 patents were issued, and their drawings are a vital reference for the beginner, enabling him to identify long-obsolete wire.

The ingenuity of the inventors is illustrated in the patent drawings reproduced here. At right, Abram V. Wormley's Y-Barb had a sheet-metal barb folded through "two or more separate strands of wire twisted together." Kittelson's patent *(below)* was for a barb knotted around a strand of two-strand cable, while the grooved cable of Dobbs's wire *(below, right)* received the barb. On the facing page at top left, a wire designed by Elijah Sims twisted two flat wires, one saw-toothed, while to its right, Merrill's Twirl offered several ways to form the barb. At bottom left on the facing page is W. T. Burrows' Joined Diamond in a two-strand version (a four-strand version is shown on page 129). At far right bottom is another diamond barb, known as Kelley's Cast Barb.

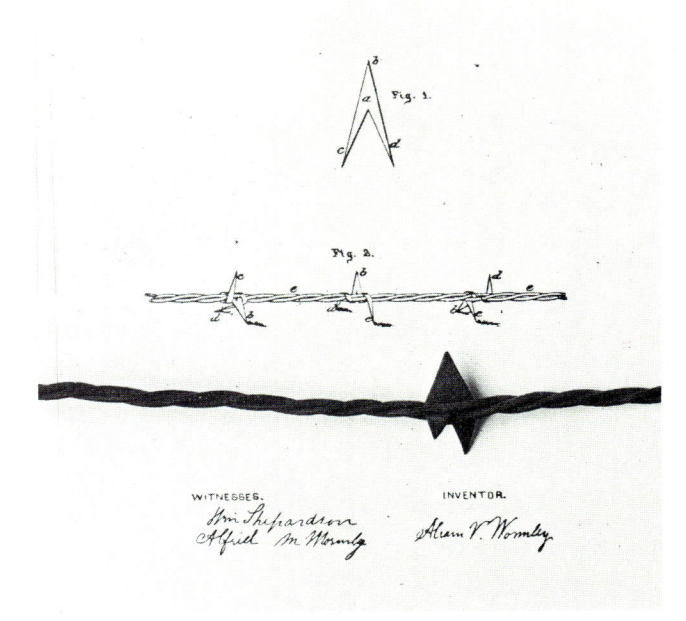

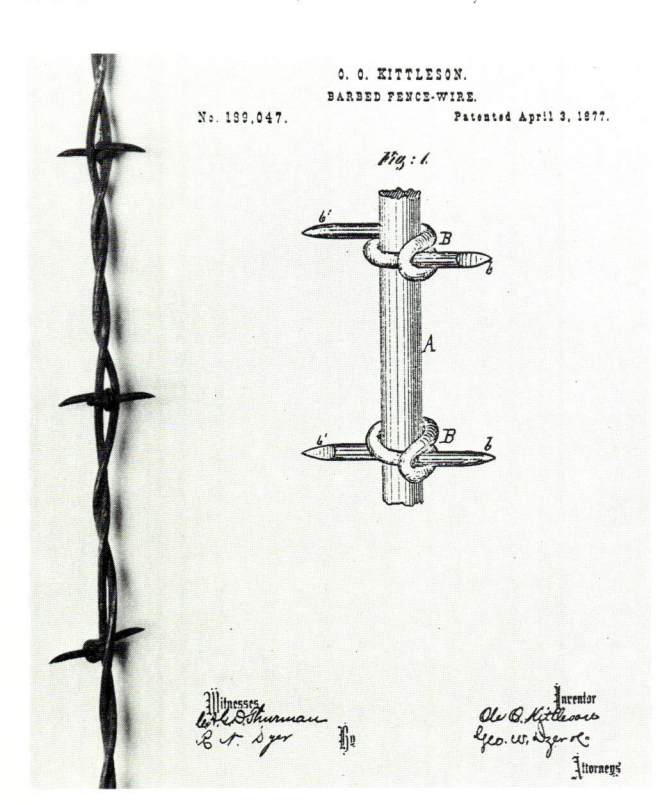

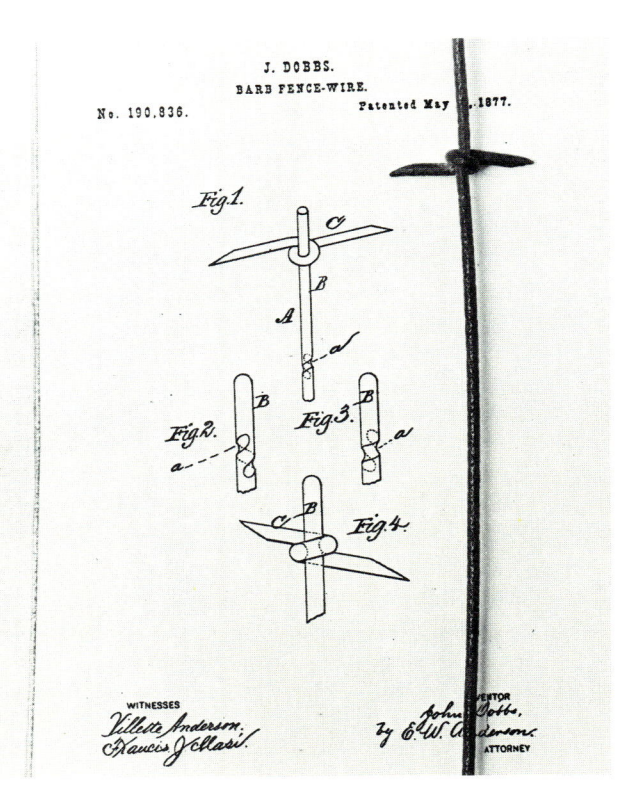

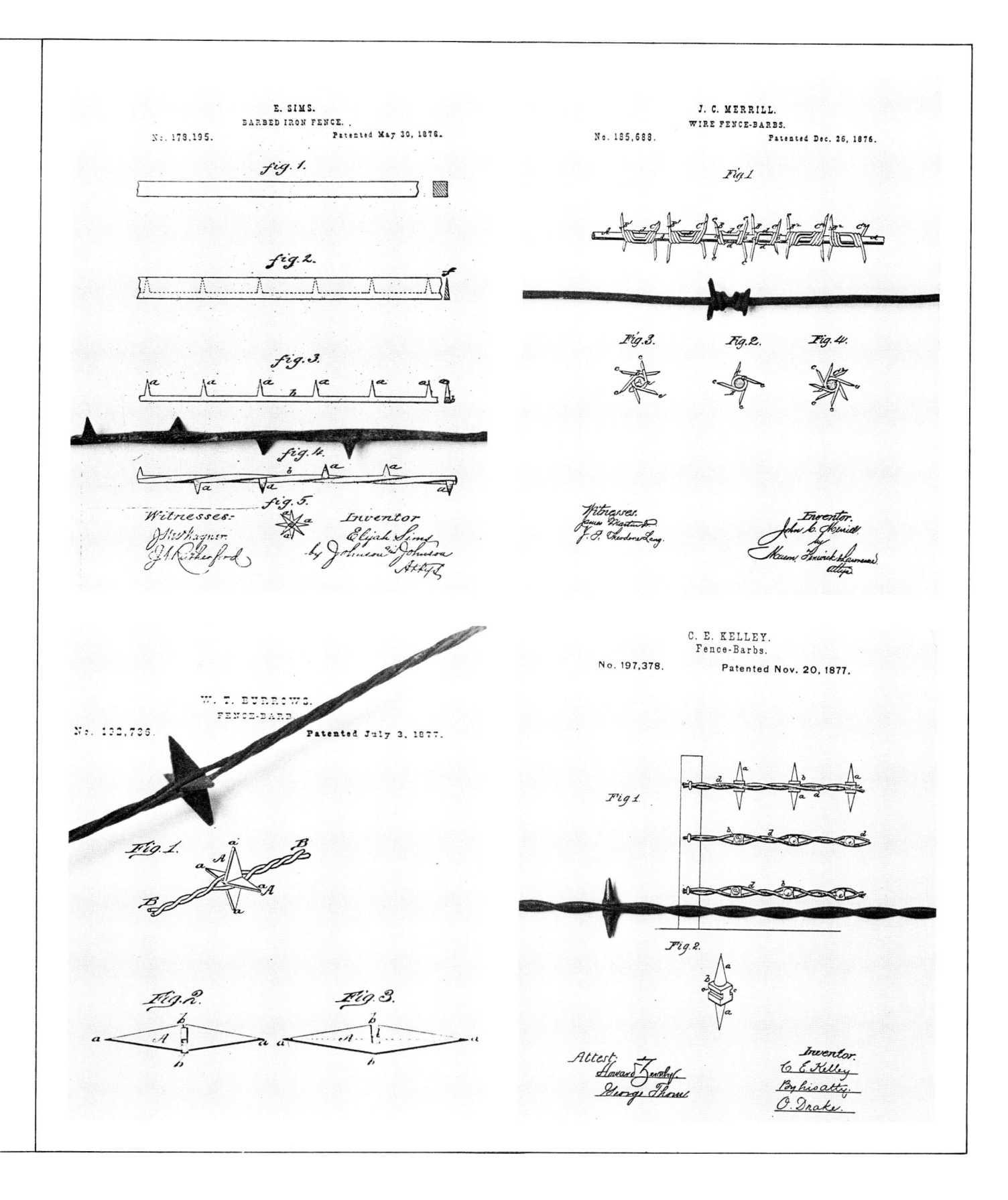

BARBED WIRE / 131

Some barbed-wire designs were more humane than others. These three wires, called "obvious fencing," were meant to be so visible to cattle that they would stay away from the fence. Scutt's Wooden Block, top, alternated plates and barbs; on the other two types, called Stubb's Plate, the plates themselves were barbed. Obvious fencing fell into disuse around 1885 because it was expensive to produce.

gallop around the corral in the night, shooting guns and brandishing flaming torches to arouse the cattle. By morning there were hide, hair and even horns hanging all over the fence. But the cattle, though they had broken one post in their stampede, were still inside.

Gates walked off with a tubful of money and invited the ranchers to San Antonio's Menger Hotel, where he bought drinks for everyone. Then he proceeded to make a pitch for his fence, proclaiming it to be light as air, cheap as dirt and as strong as good whiskey. Right there in the bar of the Menger, he sold a whole carload.

The wire that Gates huckstered with such success was the twisted barbed type familiar today. But the story of wire fencing in the West properly begins with a smooth wire—that is, nonbarbed and single strand—patented by a Texan named W. H. Meriwether in 1853. It is still possible to find pieces of Meriwether wire, and collectors prize it for its historical significance. Single-strand wire, whether it was barbed or not, normally had one critical disadvantage: extremes of hot and cold weather, which caused it to expand and contract, ultimately weakened and broke it. To overcome this defect, Meriwether's wire was manufactured in a vertical wave pattern that permitted it to adapt to changes in temperature. Like any single-strand wire, however, Meriwether's rippling "Snake" wire could be easily broken by cattle charging into it.

Government records reveal that in the years immediately following the granting of Meriwether's patent, other patents were issued to protect several types of barbed wire. However, it seems that none of these early barbed wires was manufactured in any appreciable quantity; certainly none has been found—a fact that continues to add zest to wire hunting.

The first wire to be manufactured in abundance was patented in 1868 by Michael Kelly of New York. Like many early barbed wires it was sometimes sold as dog and cat wire, to keep pets out of flowerbeds. As the first in its field, Kelly's wire is a prized exhibit in many collections. Then, in 1874, Joseph F. Glidden of Illinois patented a double strand of barbed fencing material strong enough to withstand the effects of expansion and contraction as well as the charge of maddened cattle. It was Glidden's wire, dubbed The Winner, that super-salesman Gates so effectively sold.

Glidden devised machines in which a short wire was wound around a long strand and cut off at intervals, leaving about an inch on each end to form the barb. A second strand was then twisted around the first to lock the barb in place. This scheme set the pattern followed thereafter, although many variations were achieved—by using more than two barbs; by winding the barb once, twice or more around the cable; by adding refinements like "rowels," or spurs, which are revolving metal disks with sharp points; by changing the spacing of the barbs along the cable; by altering the length of the barbs or the gauge of the cable. As a variant, wood blocks were introduced between the strands of wire to make the fencing more visible to cattle. And in place of the round wire commonly used, a flat ribbon wire was sometimes employed. In some cases ribbon wire was also twisted into cables, but the barbs in ribbon wire were generally formed by cutting into the ribbon.

Altogether, between 1868 and 1900, 756 patents were

Ornamental wire —made primarily for enclosing front yards and cemeteries—was sometimes sold with the suggestion that barbs be attached to the wire if desired to create a livestock fence. Among these dual-purpose wires were, left to right, Kilmer's wire board, intended as the name suggests to be used in lieu of a board fence; Preston's braid; Wright's spiral line; Shellaberger's snake wire; and two ribbon wires, the first nameless, the second known as Allis crimp ribbon.

Joseph Glidden produced many variations in the design of wire made under his original patent, granted in 1874. His first patent covered a design he improvised by using a coffee mill to bend a small wire into an eye that, when snipped and wrapped around a strand, formed a barb. A second strand was then twisted round to prevent the barb from slipping along the wire. In his constant search for improvements, as the examples at left show, he sometimes combined cable strands of different gauges, twisted them in varying degrees, set barbs at different distances and joined the barbs in various ways.

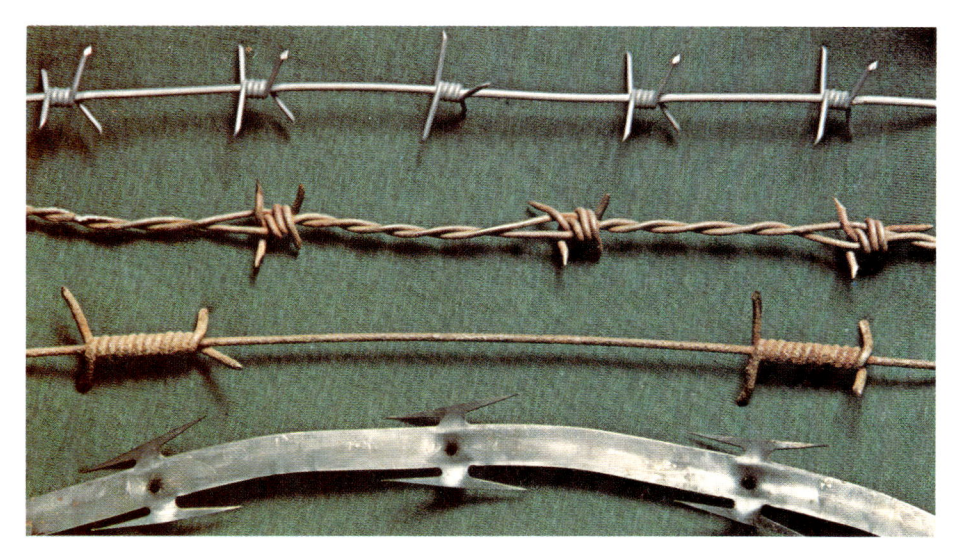

Military entanglement wire, left, was sometimes substituted for regular cattle wire, perhaps because it could be bought cheaply after World War I as surplus. Barbed wire that was designed for battlefield use was often made of a heavier gauge than cattle wire. Generally it had four-point barbs that were longer than ordinary barbs. Like cattle wire, it came in many different varieties, of which these four are typical.

Fencers' Paraphernalia

According to a Texas adage, a barbed-wire fence is of no value unless it is "horse high, bull strong and pig tight." To achieve that ideal, special tools were created to install the wire—stretch it taut as it was being put up, take up the slack when it sagged from the weight of animals or broken posts, and splice it together again when it broke or was cut by cattlemen driving their stock through to a water hole.

The fencing tools shown here, all dating from the late 19th Century, are from the collection of Bill Marquis of Ponder, Texas. Eight of them are tighteners and one is a stretcher, a type of tool that Marquis calculates produced more patents than any other kind; he has seen patent drawings for at least 50.

Fencing tools were designed to be compact and light enough for the fence mender to carry comfortably on his horse as he rode on his inspection tours. Most were crude ratchet or spring devices.

For all their efficiency, fencing tools were not the only means employed to tighten fences. Many farmers substituted a horse and wagon. By attaching a strand of wire to one spoke of a wagon wheel and urging the horse gently forward, they got the same result.

All of the objects above were invented to do the same job: take up slack in existing fences. Most, like the Spider (top center) and Birdwing (top right), were attached to the wire and turned with a tool, pliers for example, tightening the wire and locking it with a ratchet action. But some, like the one at bottom, were simple tension springs.

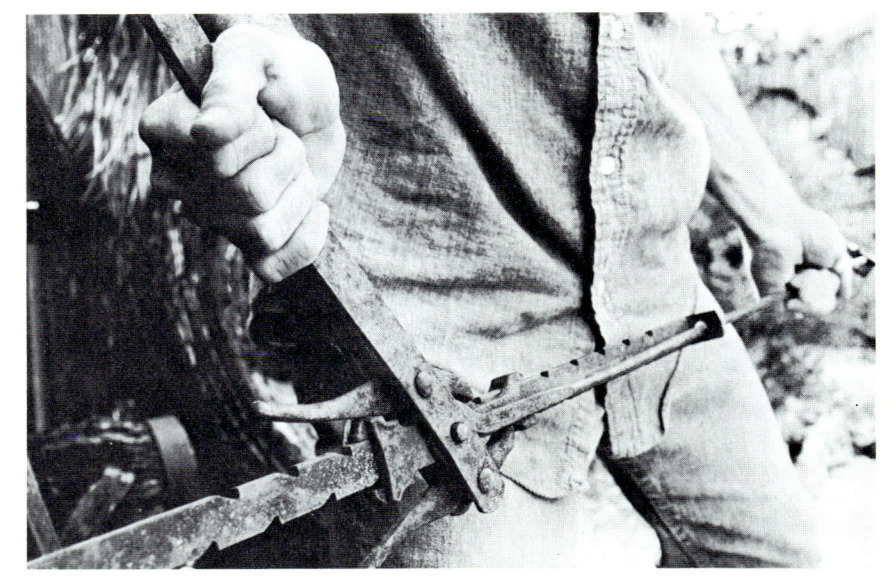

The Upham stretcher, above, was a tool used to keep the wire taut while it was being installed. It works like an automobile jack. As the handle is pumped, it moves from notch to notch to pull on the wire.

BARBED WIRE / 135

This 1877 advertisement for the famed Glidden barbed wire extols its durability and its usefulness in keeping cattle off railroad tracks.

granted for barbed wire, and examples of about 700 have been found by collectors. But since some manufacturers never bothered about patents at all, wire collections may include as many as 1,000 different types.

Suits for patent infringement clogged the courts in the last quarter of the 19th Century. Because barbed wire was easy to produce, small companies made handsome short-term profits running one step ahead of court injunctions. For a while salesman Gates floated his wire-manufacturing equipment back and forth across the Mississippi River at St. Louis, dodging the law but making a quick buck on either bank. Today only five designs are still produced; they derive from the original patents of Baker, Burnell, Curtis, Glidden and Ross.

I knew nothing of this technological history when I became a wire collector. My interest in wire grew out of a longtime fascination with the way of life of my ancestors, who came to Texas in a covered wagon. I like to give talks on the history of those early days, and one day a man in the audience invited me to see his barbed-wire collection. Now I had seen barbed wire all my life and as

The salesmanship of "Bet-a-Million" Gates, who proved that barbed wire would endure stampeding cattle, is depicted in this painting.

Collector-author "Smokey" Doyle pauses at a barbed-wire fence in a Texas field with a noncollecting companion. "I'm hard pressed to decide when I'm happier," he says, "showing my collection to friends or tramping through fields in search of new finds."

a kid growing up in Fort Worth I guess I crawled over and under thousands of barbed-wire fences. Yet here were several hundred different kinds of barbed wire, most of which I had never seen before. And when this collector began to talk to me about his wire, telling me stories of such things as the fence-cutting wars in Texas and New Mexico, suddenly it seemed as though barbed wire was directly related to the history and development of the entire West. I was hooked, and began accumulating the pieces of twisted steel that have taken up more of my time than I care to admit.

Every collector has his favorites. Mine tend to be wire I have found myself. I have one particular piece of Scutt's Wood Block I am especially fond of. It's not particularly rare or expensive—I could have bought a "stick," an 18-inch length, for about $15—but I was obsessed with finding it on my own. Several times I heard that someone had seen a Scutt's Wood Block fence a hundred miles or so away, and I would drive over just on the chance it was there. One of these trips took me to a ranch in south Texas. The rancher himself was not the kind of man who likes strangers on his land—he had been having trouble with rustlers—but he was so intrigued with my story that he gave me permission to search. And there, finally, was my Scutt's Wood Block. The trouble was that most of it was disintegrated or was lying on the ground, overgrown with grass.

I guess I followed that fence for two hours before I finally spotted a section, complete and intact, in the midst of a hedgerow of *bois d'arc,* or Osage orange, a kind of thorny tree so dense that people use it for cattle fencing. I went right into that thorny bush and when I came out I looked as if I had been crawling through barbed wire fences for 200 yards. But it was worth it.

The hunt in the open range—tedious and wearing as it may be—intrigues most collectors. Contrary to what you might think, there is still a lot of barbed wire to be found. Recently, a young friend beginning a collection observed that there really was not much good wire around any more. He believed that most of the collectible wire had been picked up. I took him through a vacant field he crossed every day on his way to school, and pulled five different kinds of wire from that one field. He had just not searched carefully enough.

There is a strict code of behavior for taking such pieces of barbed wire, however, and it is enforced by barbed-wire associations. For example, if a member were to come across an old fence where the wire was off the post and lying on the ground, he would not cut that fence. He would first determine who owned the property, find the owner, and identify himself as a member of a wire-collecting association. If the owner said that he intended to put the wire back up on the fence, the collector would offer to bring in new wire and restring the section he wanted to cut out.

This rule is not just a matter of ethics. Wire cutting is still a felony in Texas.

The prohibition against cutting a fence is not the only legal entanglement involving barbed wire. Whenever a product is in demand, some unscrupulous person will counterfeit it. Wire is no exception; counterfeiters prey on collectors. Barbed wire can be altered by adding barbs, by changing the position of the barbs and by giving the cable a different twist. Twisted wire can be straightened to become a parallel wire, straight wire can be twisted around itself to simulate a new find. Parts of different wires have been combined to form a totally "new" wire. If in doubt, compare the wire to a stick of wire you know to be legitimate. Sometimes a counterfeit may be detected by the way the barb is put on, or by a lack of rust under the newly placed barbs. If wire has been chemically aged by being buried in lime, this can often be detected by the way it is pitted. Also look to see how recently the ends of the wire were cut.

The best protection against buying counterfeit wire is to deal with people you can trust—and to be wary of bargains. Barbed-wire prices rise and fall as the supply of a particular wire is depleted or another find is made. The *International Barbed Wire Gazette* publishes a listing of "trend trade prices"—the average prices of various types as reported by 10 knowledgeable collectors across the country. One type they consistently report as high priced is Dodge Star, made by a method patented by Thomas H. Dodge of Massachusetts in 1881. His invention provides for a way to secure rowels to a wire fence so that the rowel spins in place. In 1977, Dodge Star was worth $350 per stick. When I find a piece of it for my collection, I think I'll hang up my own spurs.

Attached to posts and vertical supporting wires, finials added a touch of ornamentation to starkly utilitarian barbed-wire fences and also functioned as warning devices, making the fence more visible to cattle. The three lightweight maple-leaf designs from Canada (top) were stamped from sheet metal and have slotted bases through which the wire was threaded. The four heavier finials are made of cast iron and were manufactured in New York state for use in the West; they are pegged at the bottom for hammering into the tops of wood posts.

MUSEUMS
National Cowboy Hall of Fame and Western Heritage Center
Oklahoma City, Oklahoma 73111

COLLECTORS ORGANIZATIONS
California Barbed Wire Collectors Association
1046 North San Carlos
Porterville, California 93257

International Barbed Wire Collectors Association
c/o Bill Marquis
Route 1
Ponder, Texas 76259

Land of Lincoln Barbed Wire Collectors Association
11825 South Harding
Chicago, Illinois 60555

Texas Barbed Wire Collectors Association
1902 Boland
Capperas, Texas 76522

Wichita Barbed Wire Collectors Association
1832 South Battin
Wichita, Kansas 67202

BOOKS
McCallum, Frances T. and Henry D., *The Wire That Fenced the West.* University of Oklahoma Press, 1965.

Marquis, Bill, *The Fencin' Tool Bible, an Illustrated Guide to Identification and Classification of Fencing Tools and Related Items.* Bill Marquis, 1976.

CAPT. JACK GLASSCOCK.

J. SCHAEFER.

JOSEPH MULVEY.

CHARLES COMISKEY.

Baseball Cards
Four Generations of Heroes

The scene is etched in memory. The pick-up baseball game in the hot summer afternoon ended, and you went without hesitation to the drugstore that was somehow always situated across the street from the vacant lot in which the game was played. There you acquired a slab of gum and a pack of baseball cards. You shoved the tasteless confection into your mouth and anxiously began looking through the cards in the "nickel pack," hoping you would find one of the superstars you needed for your collection, like Joe DiMaggio, maybe, or Ted Williams. Sometimes Joe D. would show up, and you raced home to add him to a growing hoard in a cigar box that was in a bottom

Bert Randolph Sugar, author of "The Sports Collectors Bible" and other books on sports, has over 5,000 baseball cards. He also collects players' autographs, admission tickets, bats and team pennants.

bureau drawer, where he would rest safely in company with the likes of Stan Musial and Phil Cavarretta.

That's how it was, growing up in the '30s or the '40s—and even in the '50s. Bubble-gum cards were a window on the world of sport, a world in which every boy vicariously shared excitement, achievement and fame with his heroes.

If you grew up in Washington, D.C., during the late '40s and early '50s, as I did, you were obliged to look for baseball excitement in cards, for the local team, year after year, lived up to an unflattering adage: "Washington—first in war, first in peace and last in the American League." Every day you could look for the team standings in the paper and locate the Senators instantly. They were always last.

The cards of the Washington Senators depreciated in value like the German mark after World War I. The going rate for a superstar card became two, then three and, finally, four cards of the hapless Senators. You no

A page from the catalogue, circa 1889, of Allen & Ginter, the Richmond, Virginia, tobacco company that issued some of the first baseball cards, shows three of the 10 baseball players in its first set—and a billiard player. Allen & Ginter also used pictures of oarsmen, rifle shooters, pugilists, wrestlers, high jumpers, weight lifters, lawn-tennis players, hammer throwers and "pedestrians."

longer had to look up the standings in the paper. You were able to calibrate the team's position by the number of cards you would have to swap to get just one DiMaggio, Williams or Musial.

As the Washington team slipped farther in the win-loss column, so did loyalty to their cards and even to their league. No longer did you eschew cards featuring National Leaguers; nor did you view with distaste cards of New York Yankees. Rather, you became ecumenical in preference and sought out all of the players' cards as you joined the line that inevitably formed outside the drugstore after school on Mondays, when the new shipment of Bowman's gum arrived.

Everyone tried his best to build up the biggest collection of baseball cards on the block. At any given moment you knew exactly what you had and what was missing, and you rememorized the collection night after night in case you accidentally ran into someone willing to trade a hard-to-get card.

Every school recess, every luncheon period—in fact, seemingly every waking minute—was given to cards. You could approach any of the neighborhood kids, even one with whom you had only a nodding acquaintanceship, and hand him your cigar box filled with "dupes." In turn, he handed you his. Then you meticulously went through each other's collections while reciting the standard litany—"got-it-got-it-need-it-got-it-got-it-need-it." Finally, familiar with what each had to offer, you got down to the business of swapping.

My own lifelong love affair with the sport of baseball was initiated by the proximity of my house to Griffith Stadium in Washington, D.C., just a trolley-car ride away. Every afternoon I jumped aboard a car after cutting classes—or more accurately, hung onto the back of it for a free ride—and was able, through the kindness of two lovable old gatekeepers, to stroll into the stadium by paying them with only a smile and a friendly wave of the hand. Before long I began collecting baseball cards and have continued ever since, gradually building up a collection of some 5,000.

In the provinciality of my teen-age years, it never occurred to me that card collecting and swapping were being carried on all over the country. A kindred spirit then unknown to me was Bill Himmelman, who was

140 / BASEBALL CARDS

On an early card, plugging Old Judge cigarettes in the 1880s, "Germany" Long poses catching a ball hung on a string.

The first card in color, celebrating fielder Jack Nelson of the old New York Mets, was issued in the 1880s by Gold Coin cigarettes.

Another rarity from the pre-1900 period pictures Mike Kelly of Boston, who inspired the cry "Slide, Kelly, slide."

Frank "Home Run" Baker, third baseman for the Philadelphia Athletics, stares from a 1908 card that lists the city and the league.

John McGraw, who led the Giants to pennant after pennant, appears on a 1909 card, one of few honoring managers.

On a card issued in 1920, before bats were standardized in shape, Heinie Groh of Cincinnati wields his "bottle" club.

BASEBALL CARDS / 141

The Rarest Card of all

WAGNER, PITTSBURG

The rectitude that shines from the stern visage of Honus Wagner is genuine—and makes this card worth $3,000 and up. It is known as T-206, after its number in the distributor's listing; only 19 are known to exist. The card was part of a set of 561 issued in 1910 by the American Tobacco Company. Honus Wagner, the star shortstop of the Pittsburgh Pirates, objected to smoking and did not want to be linked with tobacco. He successfully sued to enjoin American Tobacco from using his likeness and name.

Another card in the same series is worth at least $1,000. This is Eddie Plank's card. The printing plate broke during the production run and so this Philadelphia Athletics player is commemorated by only 25 pasteboards.

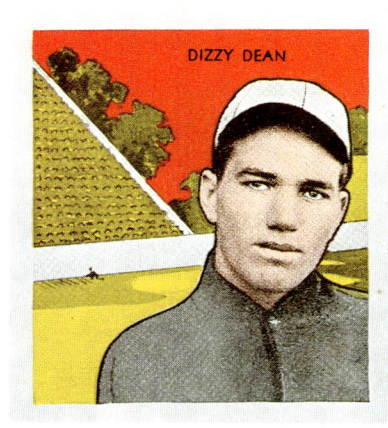

From the prized 1933-1941 period is this picture of Dizzy Dean of the St. Louis Cardinals, given away with Tattoo-Orbit gum.

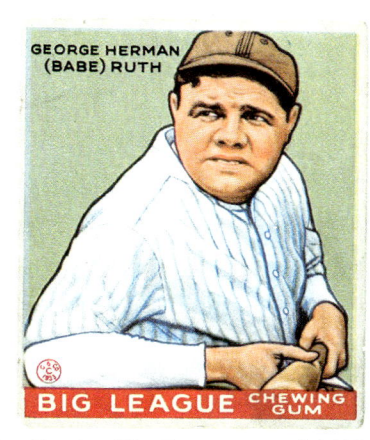

The Goudey Big League set of 1933 includes Babe Ruth, whose card was worth more than $40 by the late 1970s.

Ice-cream-cup lids as well as gum cards featured ballplayers in the '30s. Above, on a 1937 lid, is Bob Feller of Cleveland.

The Goudey Heads Up set of 1938 has a picture of the player's head—Joe DiMaggio in this case—atop a caricature of his body.

Action pictures of the 1940 Play Ball set include hitter Ted Williams, Al Schacht— known for his pregame antics–and umpire Dolly Stark, one of the few shown on a card.

Among many novelty cards is the 1935 Big League Puzzle card. Each has four photographs on one side and part of another on the reverse. The back is aligned with related pieces to make a big picture.

growing up 300 miles north in Teaneck, New Jersey.

Himmelman was all of nine years old when he saw his first baseball card. He came to collecting cards so late in life because none were being made when he was younger, during World War II. But he made up for the time he had lost. His collection has since become one of the largest in the country, with more than 100,000 different cards, many of them rarities. From Himmelman's collection have been selected the illustrations that were used for this article.

Although Himmelman and I did not become acquainted with each other until we were deeply involved with baseball cards as adults, our youthful collecting experiences were similar in many respects. For one thing, neither of us stuck with the avocation continuously from boyhood. During our teen years we discovered cars and then girls; in the meantime, our baseball cards gathered dust in bureau drawers.

When we came home after college, we found the collections of our childhood preserved by our mothers as if in a time capsule. The rediscovery of those 2½-by-3½-inch pasteboards awakened remembrance of a time past. I subscribed once again to a publication that I had taken 11 years earlier. Occasionally it offered baseball cards for sale.

At the same time, Bill Himmelman encountered a neighbor who had collected something called Play Ball cards in the late '30s and early '40s. They were the first cards Himmelman saw other than the Bowmans and Leafs of his childhood. Then we noticed, in the pages of LIFE, a beautiful four-color feature article about cards of the early 1900s. And finally, we separately came across a listing of auction prices for baseball cards, called the Card Collector's Bulletin, that was put out by Charles Bray of Bangor, Pennsylvania.

Each of us responded to a small advertisement in a sports weekly—so small that it would have been overlooked by anyone except those who read the paper from cover to cover—and sent away for the most recent edition of the Bray listing. Himmelman sat with it for hours on end. I took it with me to my job and spent more time poring over it than I did over work. Like brides-to-be with their "wish books," we both became absorbed in a world of baseball cards we had never dreamed of. It was a world, we discovered, that dated back to the 1880s and had been divided by collectors into five historical periods.

The first period started with the issuance of baseball cards by Goodwin & Company to promote their cigarettes. It was the 1880s, and a great cigarette war was raging. Goodwin had earlier issued cards with pictures of various 19th Century American types—police captains, show girls, bicyclists, prize fighters and Indian chiefs. Now, since baseball was after all the national pastime, Goodwin began turning out cards depicting heroes of the diamond with every package of Old Judge cigarettes, and with another brand, Gypsy Queen. The cards were small—1¾ by 2¾ inches—and sepia colored. The players came into a studio and posed for the pictures, standing perfectly motionless, with hands or bat extended toward a ball hanging by a very visible string from the ceiling.

In time, other cigarette companies joined in. Allen & Ginter and D. Buchner put out beautifully colored cards. P. H. Mayo & Bro. Tobacco Company produced black-and-white cards. All of these cards were intended to further the sales of cigarettes now long gone and forgotten. This period ended around the turn of the century, when the monopolistic American Tobacco Company, which had been established through a series of mergers, either acquired or put out of business nearly all independent cigarette manufacturers. There was no longer any competition for sales and thus no further need for sales-promoting gimmicks like picture cards.

But a few years later the Sherman Anti-Trust Act took effect, and eventually the tobacco trust was broken up into separate companies. Competition revived, and with

BASEBALL CARDS / 143

This folding card, the 1912 Triplefolder, opens to display two small pictures and one large one. Above, Ty Cobb and George Moriarity— the only man to become a major-league player, manager and umpire—flank a shot of Moriarity at third base.

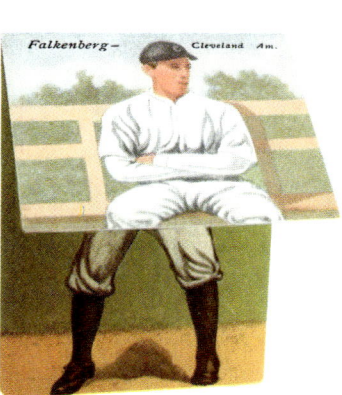

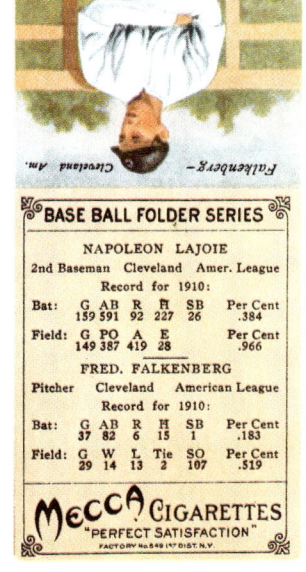

On the front of the 1911 Doublefolder is a full-length picture of Napoleon LaJoie of the Cleveland Naps (far left). On the back is the torso of Fred Falkenberg (far right). When the card is folded (center), the torso matches LaJoie's legs to give a second full picture.

National Favorites in Limited Edition

Especially valued by many collectors are the cards that originated in limited editions, as premiums included with new products—such as bread, dog food, cookies, chewing tobacco—that were being test-marketed in selected areas of the country. When the products eventually were distributed nationwide, so were the cards, but collectors nevertheless continue to call them regionals because they started that way.

Johnston's Cookies cards of Milwaukee Braves marked the first three years of the franchise in that city.

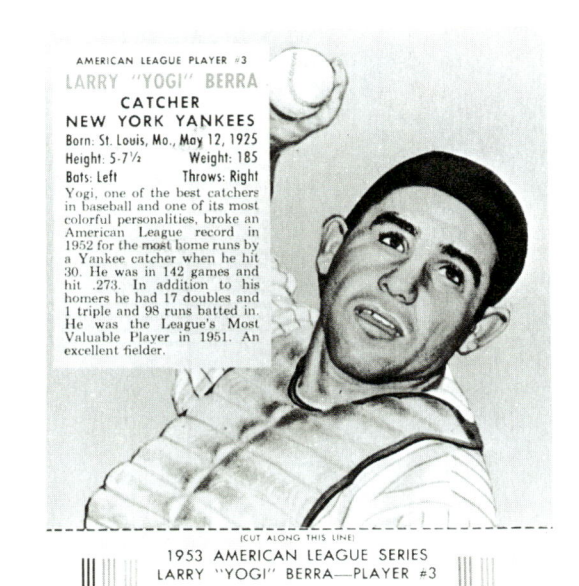

Yogi Berra is featured on an outsized card—3¼ by 4 inches—that was issued by Red Man tobacco.

Red Heart Dog Food distributed 33 cards of such Yankee stars as Billy Martin and Mickey Mantle in 1954.

Joe Garagiola and John Berardino appear on cards for St. Louis teams in a 1947 set plugging Tip Top bread.

it came the second period of baseball cards. New sets of baseball cards began to appear, promoting such exotically named brands as El Principe de Wales, Fatima, Fez, Hassan, Mecca, Hindu, Sweet Caporals and Tolstoi. There was also a cigarette named Ty Cobb; this star was the only ballplayer to have a brand of cigarette named for him. In all, more than 200 brand names were advertised by small cards, most bearing a head-and-shoulders shot of a player. Some were ingeniously constructed to be double- or even triple-folded so as to show more than one player per card.

Not only were the major leaguers featured. Minor-league players, from teams in Shreveport, Montgomery, Nashville and even Danville, Virginia, also were enshrined. Several nontobacco companies got into the act. Cracker Jack popcorn, Tip Top bread and *Sporting Life* magazine all brought out cards of their own. Thus collectors were given a cornucopia of cards that covered the period up through 1915.

The third period followed directly after the second, and is marked by a sharp drop in the technical quality of the cards. Around 1916, World War I cut off the supply of German-made printing ink pigments to the American manufacturers, who then had to make do with inferior ones. Even after the War was over, the quality remained low, and most of the cards of this era, from 1916 to 1932, are relatively unattractive. They were printed in tints of yellow, green or blue.

During this period so-called exhibit cards came to be popular; they were larger, about postcard-size, and were sometimes dispensed in strips from machines. The cards that were produced during this time are not as much in demand among collectors simply because they are less attractive than those issued earlier or later.

The next period, which lasted from 1933 through 1941, when the United States entered World War II, was best known for the birth of cards as they are known today. Most were given away with the purchase of bubble gum, not cigarettes. The Goudey Gum Co. and the DeLong Gum Co., both of Boston, brought out several series of cards, such as Heads Up and Lou Gehrig Says, that are prized among collectors today because of their scarcity. They were not marketed in huge quantities because this was of course the period of the Great Depression, when most American families had precious little to spend on frivolities, a category that no doubt included bubble gum.

Wartime scarcities forced a halt in the production of cards, but immediately after World War II the fifth era started. Bubble-gum cards were issued at first by Leaf Confectionery, Inc., by Bowman and by Frank H. Fleer Corp. Later and into the 1970s, they were distributed almost exclusively by the firm now most identified with baseball cards—Topps Chewing Gum, Incorporated.

In this dual-purpose Play Ball card of 1933, the picture shows Pepper Martin, credited with almost singlehandedly winning the 1931 World Series, while the back explains a pitcher's grip.

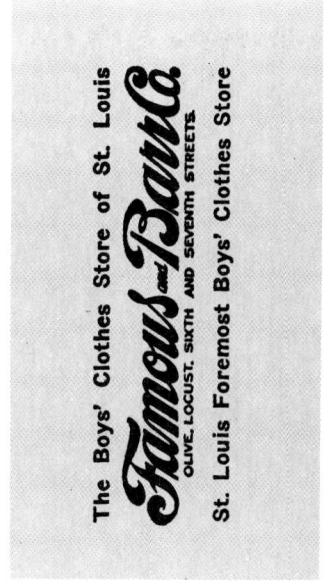

J. Erskine Mayer, pitcher for the pennant-winning Phillies of 1915, is among the players in a set of cards given away by a variety of sponsors whose advertisements appear on the back (right).

146 / BASEBALL CARDS

The 1951 Brooklyn Dodgers—among them such players as Jackie Robinson, Pee Wee Reese, Duke Snider and Don Newcombe—line up for a Topps team card. These were the players, featured in the best-selling book "The Boys of Summer," who won five pennants and one World Series in eight seasons. In 1951, however, they dramatically lost the pennant to their archrivals, the New York Giants.

Eddie Collins is one of a 1951 set in which the pictures were die-cut to stand upright.

Card Games for Collectors

One way to build a collection of baseball cards is to win it. This method is used by many young people, who can seldom afford to buy rarities, for the cards lend themselves to a variety of "flipping" games in which participants risk the cards they play with.

The simplest game, known as Matching, is played like heads-or-tails coin tossing. In Farthees the object is to flip a card farther than the other players can. In Topsies one player tries to throw his card so that it lands on top of his opponent's, and in Knock Down the Leaner he must flip his card to displace one leaning against a step. While players disagree on the more reliable techniques for winning, two "grips" for starting the cards on their flight *(right)* are widely favored.

A thumb-forefinger grip guides direction of the card most accurately.

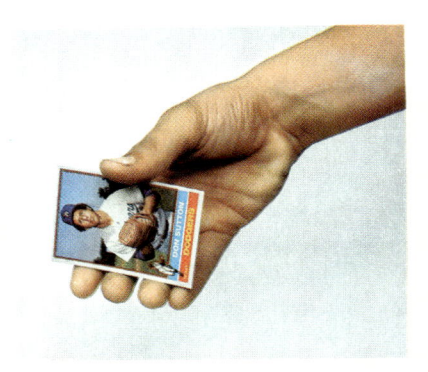

To play Matching, flip the card with a thumb and three fingers.

Cards of the 1960s such as these five, picturing (left to right) Juan Marichal, Willie Mays, Mickey Mantle, Ernie Banks, Hank Aaron and Roberto Clemente, are fairly easy for the beginning collector to locate. Although all of these players hold major pitching, batting and fielding records, and no major collection would be complete without them, some of the cards can be bought for as little as a nickel each.

When Bill Himmelman and I separately resumed our interest in collecting in the late 1950s, we picked up where we had left off. We not only collected cards; we also enjoyed studying the information they provided. The player's likeness on the front of the card was backed by a capsule of his playing career and an admirably succinct characterization of the man. (One of my favorites: "Paul Waner probably spilt more whiskey than Babe Ruth ever drank.")

Although Himmelman and I absorbed the information that was offered by the cards, we did not regard them as possessing the magic that former Houston Astros third baseman Doug Rader professed to find in them. When asked during an interview how he came to know so much about baseball, Rader said earnestly, "It came from these baseball cards." Holding one up for the camera, he proceeded to take a bite out of it, saying, "See, if you just chew up these facts on the back of the card, pretty soon you'll absorb everything there is to know about the players."

Himmelman became a particular fan of the 1930s era of baseball; I went farther back, to the turn of the century. Cards continued to provide both of us with a wealth of historical information about the game and we continued to discover new collectors—and new sources for our own collections.

Bill Himmelman and I finally met at a baseball-card convention in 1968, the first we attended and one of the earliest to be held anywhere. "It was held at another collector's house, Mike Aronstein's, and 23 collectors from all over the country attended," Himmelman remembers. The gathering provided an opportunity for us to meet other collectors and to exchange cards and gossip. This convention symbolized the movement of a hobby to the status of a nationwide phenomenon.

Since that day as many as 50 conventions a year have been held in cities all over the country and at least a dozen were major events, lasting several days and attracting up to 3,000 people each. Some conventiongoers are wide-eyed Little Leaguers carrying their collections in cardboard boxes; others are Wall Street lawyers who mount their cards in specially designed files or expensive leather versions of a salesman's sample case. All day long they wander up and down aisles lined with as many as 200 tables, buying, trading and selling, and in the evening they attend auctions of cards that have not been sold during the day.

Though the tempo of the convention is unhurried, the mood is often intense. One collector claimed he sometimes did not eat, sleep or leave the hotel during the entire convention and that the proceedings had some of the excitement of the floor of the New York Stock Exchange. Indeed, some people tend to regard their card collections as a good investment as well as a hobby. It is not unheard of for a collector to make as much as $20,000 a year simply from buying and selling baseball cards, and in 1977 one good but modest collection sold for $40,000. In fact, one of the largest collec-

Cards to Suit All Tastes

Although baseball cards today are inextricably linked with the national pastime—they did not start out that way. Allen & Ginter, the Richmond tobacco firm that issued the first ones, included pictures of pool players, boxers, oarsmen, sharpshooters and wrestlers. And a variety of sports still are represented along with baseball on the cardboard pictures included with candy, chewing gum, tobacco and even hot dogs.

Some of the picture giveaways had nothing to do with any sport, but were meant to induce purchasers to assemble collections relating to anything of current interest. Such comic-strip and cartoon-movie characters as Henry, Dick Tracy and Mickey Mouse were a natural choice to be wrapped with chewing gum and caramels intended for sale to children. But even the macabre was exploited: in the late 1930s one set of cards, called Horrors of War, depicted atrocities committed during the Japanese invasion of Manchuria.

While all these cards are sought after, and many people prefer to collect nonsport cards—a Lillian Russell was worth a dollar in the late 1970s—athletics remains the principal interest among card makers and card collectors. The choice is considerable *(below)*. There are cards honoring college football before World War I and professional football of the 1930s. Basketball, boxing and auto racing also are represented. And as early as 1910, hockey players appeared on cards that, understandably, were popular in Canada.

One of many hockey cards issued in Canada, this card pictures Archie Wilcox, a defenseman who played for the Montreal Maroons and the Boston Americans.

Knute Rockne, the fabled coach who in 13 years at Notre Dame lost only 12 of 117 football games, appears in a 1935 set of football notables of the era.

This 1958 Topps set picturing basketball players includes Sweetwater Clifton (left), one of the first blacks in the NBA, and Bill Russell of the Boston Celtics.

Included in a 1948 series honoring boxers is this picture of Sugar Ray Robinson, the middleweight who established a record of 109 knockouts.

With every purchase of a brand of hot dogs came a picture of a winner of the Indianapolis 500. Above is Troy Ruttman, one of the sport's leading moneymakers, in the Agajanian Special he drove to win in 1952.

Youthful connoisseurs examine an album of baseball cards at a convention of collectors in New York. One of many, it drew 2,500 visitors and dealers with more than two million cards.

Collector Bill Himmelman, whose cards illustrate this article, got himself on a card (above) by printing up a set for the semipro Tri Valley Highlanders: he is the team's first baseman and manager.

tions—200,000 cards—was considered so valuable by its owner, Jefferson Burdick, that he bequeathed it to New York City's Metropolitan Museum of Art in 1963. (It can be seen there by appointment; children must be accompanied by an adult, and no child less than 10 years of age is admitted.)

As baseball cards grew up from a kid's pastime, they became more than a boyhood hobby for Bill Himmelman and me. In addition to his job as head of a welding-torch company, Himmelman became the president of a store that sells sports collectibles, and he also was involved in opening a similar store in Cooperstown, New York, the cradle of baseball. I applied my interest to my profession as a writer, and spent nearly 10 years putting together a guide for baseball-card collectors called *The Sports Collectors Bible*.

For Himmelman, interest in baseball is not limited to collecting cards. He also played baseball while he was a student in high school and college. More recently he played on a semipro team, a role that gave him an opportunity for a special distinction. He arranged to have baseball cards printed up for his team, thus becoming the only known card collector to have his picture appear on a card as a player. It evokes much the same feeling in Himmelman as it did in Jim Campanis, the former Los Angeles Dodger catcher, who once said: "The only way I knew I made it to the major leagues was when I saw my picture on a baseball gum card."

MUSEUMS
Metropolitan Museum of Art, Burdick Collection
New York, New York 10028

National Baseball Hall of Fame and Museum
Cooperstown, New York 13326

BOOKS
Burdick, J. R., ed., *The American Card Catalog*. Nostalgia Press, 1967.

Clark, Steve, *The Complete Book of Baseball Cards*. Grosset and Dunlap Inc., 1976.

Douglas, John, *Sports Memorabilia*. Wallace-Homestead, 1976.

Sugar, Bert Randolph:
Classic Baseball Cards. Dover Publications, 1977.
The Sports Collectors Bible. Wallace-Homestead, 1975.

PERIODICALS
Baseball Advertiser. The Card Memorabilia Assoc., P.O. Box 2, Amawalk, New York 10501

The Trader Speaks. Dan Dishley, 3 Pleasant Drive, Lake Ronkonkoma, New York 11779

Sports Collector's Digest. John Stommen, P.O. Box E, Milan, Michigan 48160

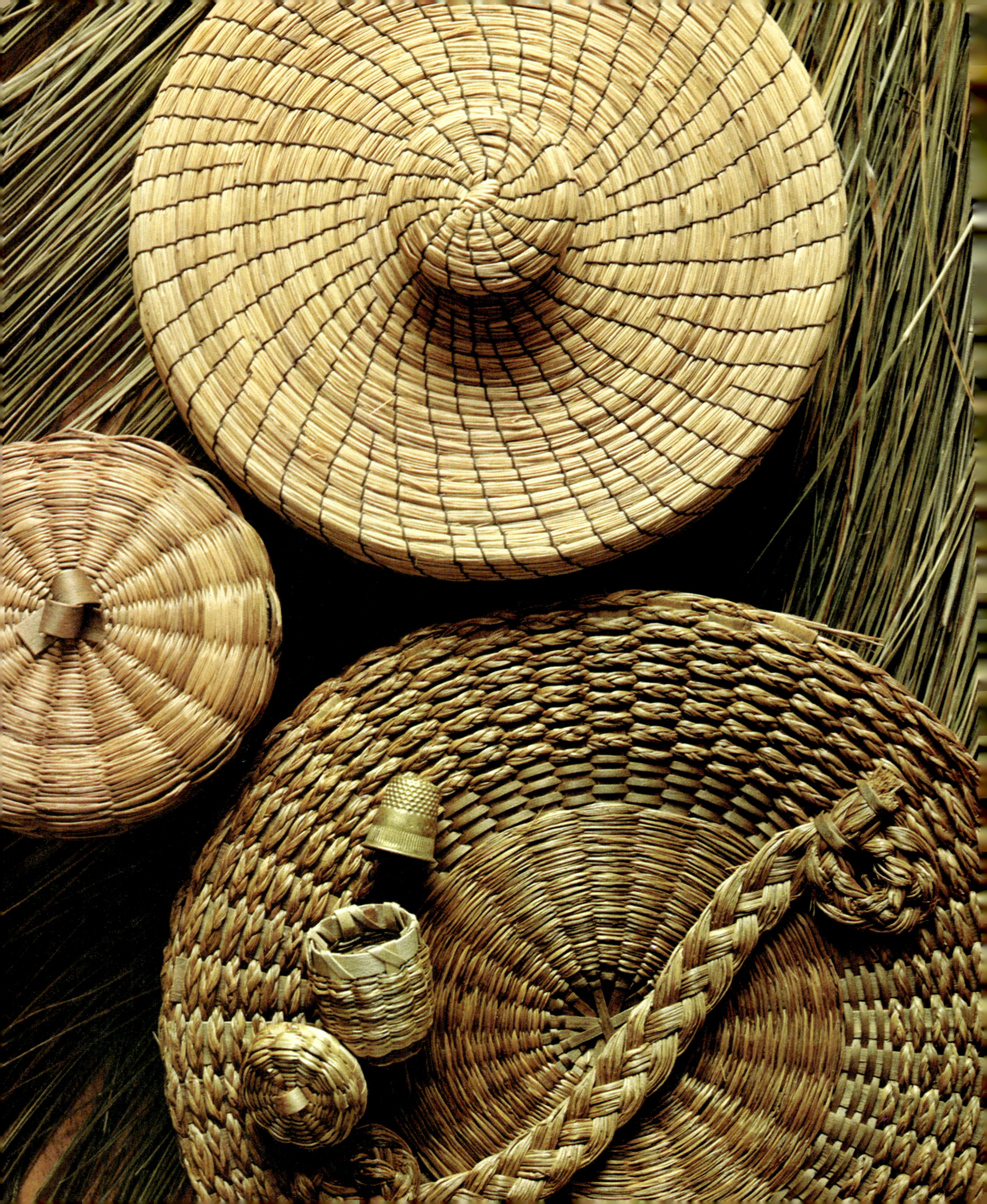

Baskets
Handy and Handsome Carryalls

For many like myself, to collect baskets is to look into America's pioneer past. In a little antique shop recently, I found a rarity, a goose basket. It cost three dollars. It is not pretty, for it is shaped like a spittoon. But it had a very special use, one that recalls American life in the days before pillows were filled with foam rubber and blankets were electrified. The basket was made to be put over a goose's head while its feathers were being plucked

Marion Burr Sober developed an interest in basketry when she studied occupational therapy, and has written extensively on the subject. She taught art in the 1950s at Wayne State University.

as filling for pillows and comforters. Geese, as you probably know, have a wicked bite.

Other baskets that bring back the America of an earlier time are the Nantucket Lightship baskets woven by sailors on long tours of duty aboard the floating lighthouse that once was anchored off the old Massachusetts whaling port. Made in nests of graduated sizes—so many per nest—of rattan woven over sturdy oak or hickory ribs, they are sometimes branded with the seagoing basketmaker's name. Nantucket Lightship baskets are among the more valuable baskets you can find. A nest of eight from any time before the 1920s could go for $4,000 or more.

The early American baskets that interest me most, however, are the ones made by Indians. In my opinion, the finest baskets in the world are coil baskets used in religious ceremonies by the Pomos, a Pacific Coast tribe. These baskets have small, fluffy feathers interwoven with the coils, and are so beautiful and rare that when one turns up for sale it may bring a fancy price, $2,500 or more. But there are other Indian baskets, less expensive and just as fascinating, such as the tightly woven baskets of grass and roots made by Southwestern tribes *(pages 158-159)*. Most were meant to hold grains and fruits, but some are so leakproof that the Indians used them for cooking,

Indian baskets made of sweet grass range in size from a strap-handled sewing basket, 12 inches across, to a tiny thimble holder. They are displayed on a bed of sweet grass.

A wicker picnic basket was once part of every American family's life. This sturdy hamper could, and did, carry all the picnic makings—food, dishes, glasses and usually a real linen tablecloth.

A 16-inch willow basket with scalloped sides makes a snug bed for a cat. The openwork design resembles the lacy pattern of an ordinary willow fruit basket, but the construction is sturdier.

152 / BASKETS

Tools of the basketmaker's art include two round wooden molds (top), on which baskets like the one in the foreground are formed, and a fan-shaped mold on which a splint basket is woven (center). The hooklike instrument by the unfinished basket is a cutting gauge. The triangular teeth embedded in its face are pulled across wide splints like those coiled at center left, to slice them into uniform strips.

filling them with a mixture of corn meal and water into which was dropped heated stones.

Good baskets can be found anywhere in this country, often far from the place where they were made. Because they were light and handy, people used them for packing, as we use cardboard boxes today. You will find Indian baskets from Maine, New Hampshire or New York in upper Michigan (where I do much of my hunting) as well as on the West Coast and in the South—Americans who retire to those regions take family possessions with them. Old baskets naturally are more valuable than new ones, but many traditional styles are still produced by traditional techniques, and you can build a fine collection of brand-new ones that are historically authentic if you know what to look for at roadside stands and craftwork markets.

Understanding how a basket is constructed will make you a shrewder, more appreciative collector. Four techniques are employed in basketry: wickerwork, twining, plaiting and coiling. And while many fibers are suitable, most baskets made in this country are woven from only

The rough texture of rye straw is revealed in this close-up of a coil basket once used by Pennsylvania Dutch housewives to hold dough.

Six outstanding baskets from the author's collection represent a range of basketry traditions. At rear is a Chippewa ash-splint basket with dyed bands of color and a movable handle. Others (from left) are a Yurok fish trap made of willow; a double-weave Cherokee basket; a Nantucket Lightship basket handbag; a Chippewa curlicue basket, thought to bring luck; and an old wicker-woven willow fruit basket.

Basic Basketry Patterns

Wickerwork, twining and two versions of plaiting are illustrated in these drawings of four common basketry techniques. All four are created by running flexible "weavers" over and under spokes, which tend to be rigid. But the weaving sequences differ, producing changes in pattern, and the patterns suit different materials—sturdy splints in some cases, soft reeds and grasses in others.

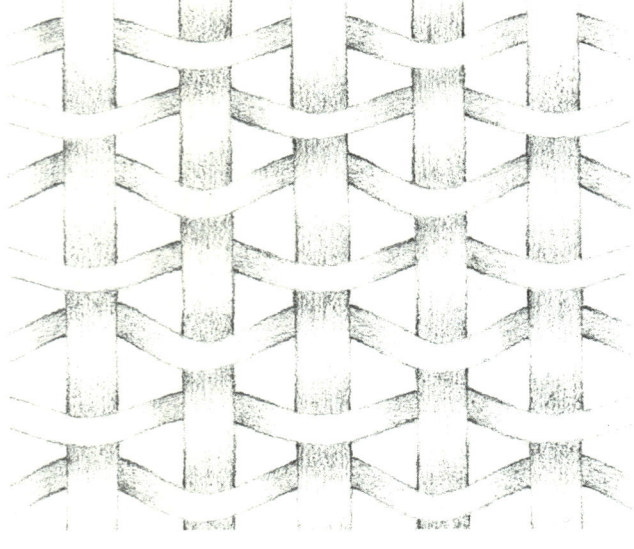

Wickerwork, a simple over-and-under technique, is the most widely used basket weave. It is also called "in and out." In the example above, weavers and spokes are the same distance apart, but this is not essential; the spokes are often widely spaced.

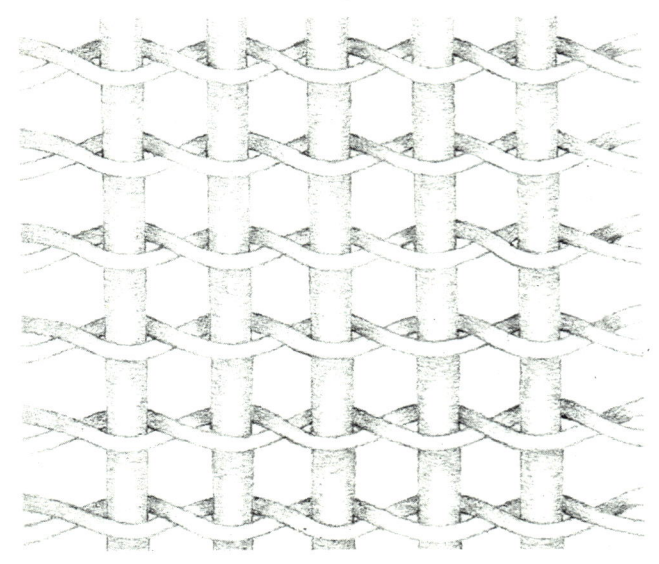

Twining is like wickerwork, except that the weavers are multiple strands, which are twisted together as they pass over the spokes so that they interlock. The weavers for twining are necessarily very flexible, and the resulting baskets are often finely woven.

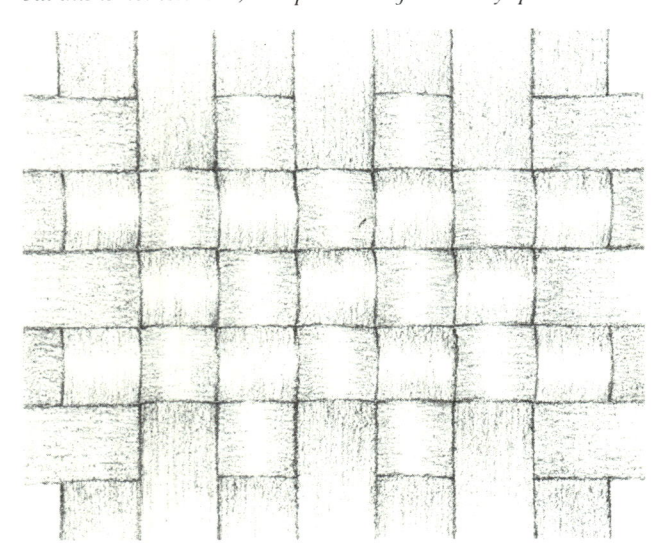

Plain plaiting, or checkerwork, can be woven with open spaces or pulled up tight, as in the example above. Weavers and spokes are generally of the same material and size, but some may be dyed different colors to heighten the checkerboard effect.

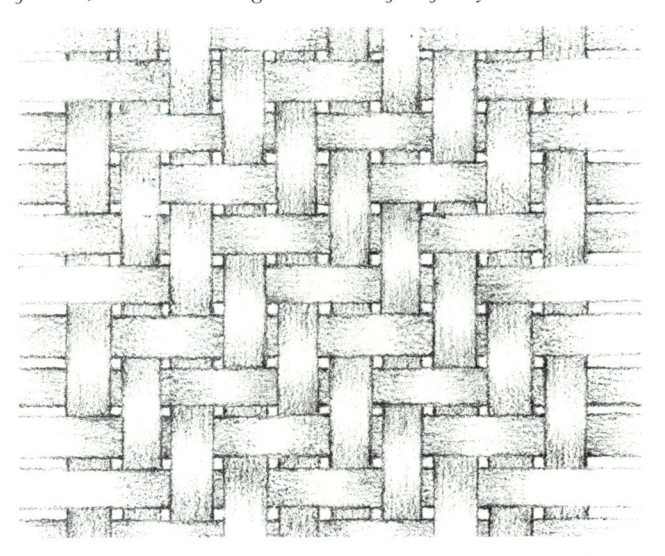

Twill plaiting, or twillwork, creates diagonal effects by staggering the bottom of the weave in each succeeding row. Various sequences are used. Here the weaver passes over two and under two spokes; another common sequence is over-two, under-one.

BASKETS / 155

Four spokes were crossed in the base of this basket as weaving began. More were inserted later as the work widened.

Two baskets recall another age in American rural life. The tall container is a goose basket, which covered the bird's head while its feathers were being plucked. The smaller basket is a child's berrypicker, easily recognizable by the fruit stains on the inside.

These variations on the standard rib-type basket all have fixed handles. In the foreground is a contemporary white oak-splint basket. The "gizzard basket" (left), which is noted for its distinctive raised central rib, was used to hold eggs and is made of hickory splint. The sturdy rib-type basket shown at right is made of white oak. The large, rough-textured basket is woven from unpeeled willow.

two grasses and the wood of five trees. The trees are young willow, hickory, black ash, white ash and white oak. The grasses are sweet grass and rye straw.

Among the easier baskets to find are willow, which is typically used to make picnic hampers, fishing creels and fruit baskets. An old-fashioned willow fruit basket with the ribs forming scalloped loops around the rim can be acquired for a few dollars and is a good beginning purchase for a novice collector. Willow baskets are made of branches cut in the spring before the sap rises. In most cases, these branches are peeled and soaked in water before weaving, although sometimes a basket is roughly made with unpeeled wood. Willow baskets show their age readily. New willow is tan and shiny; old willow is straw colored with a mat finish.

For baskets made of hickory or white oak, the wood is first split into flexible strips called splints. In splinting, the tree is felled, split into quarters and eighths, then separated lengthwise along its growth rings. These pieces are then pulled apart by hand, sometimes with the help of a knife, into long, thin strips. Finally the strips, or splints, are repeatedly smoothed. In splint baskets, it is fairly easy to see the differences between the woods when the baskets are new. As they age, it becomes harder to tell. Ordinarily white ash is smooth and light in color; black ash is nut-brown. Hickory and white oak are silvery gray, but hickory has a close, even grain while the grain of white oak is more uneven and widely separated.

Sweet-grass baskets, as fragrant as their name implies, are made from a wide-stalked, low-growing plant of the Northeast and the Great Lakes region. It is harvested in the spring and cured over heat until it curls into thin strands for weaving. The sweet aroma of the grass used to hang over the loads of these baskets that Indians brought into Northeastern towns early in this century. Even now, if you dampen an old sweet-grass basket you can smell the perfume. The Chippewa of Michigan still specialize in sweet-grass baskets; so do the Penobscot of Maine and the Micmacs of Nova Scotia.

The straw of the rye plant is an old basketry favorite in both Europe and America. The straw is harvested when ripe, then trimmed and soaked in water until the stalks are pliable enough to be twisted into coils. Usually the coils are woven together with hickory bark or cord. In Pennsylvania Dutch households, rye-straw baskets were used for holding bread dough overnight, while it was rising, as well as for storing grain and for conical beehives called skeps.

In addition to the standard woods and grasses, any number of materials were used regionally. In the southern Appalachians, honeysuckle vines were, and are, used for Indian basketry. Corn shucks were popular in the Midwest; long, thick pine needles in the South.

Some Indians tenderized tree roots—some of which grow 30 to 40 feet long—by chewing them. You may also find Indian baskets of sumac, yucca, the inner bark of cedar, and palm leaves.

A particularly scarce but valuable basket fiber called river cane is harvested from a very small area around Cherokee, North Carolina. Here the Cherokee weavers, achieving an ancestral pattern by a technique not divulged to outsiders, fashion the river cane into double-weave baskets—two baskets in one, both made in the same continuous process. When tightly woven, they are capable of carrying water.

Whatever the material, the most frequently used and simplest weave in basketry is the wicker, or over-and-under, weave *(diagrams, page 154)*. Wickerwork baskets are made in many styles. In wickerwork splint baskets the splints provide a broad, flat surface suitable for decorations like the colorful ovals and stars that embellish the "potato stamp" baskets *(bottom right)* of the Iroquois and Algonquian Indians.

Designs are also incorporated into rib-type wickerwork baskets. For this type, two hoops are bound together at right angles, one forming the basket handle, the other the rim. Curving spokes are then inserted into two tightly wrapped joints to form a framework resembling the human rib cage. Lovely patterns can be woven into the sides of these baskets, and one kind has an especially ingenious shape. These rib-type baskets, called gizzard baskets for their fancied resemblance to a chicken gizzard *(page 155)*, have a divided bottom, formed by the two rounded halves meeting in the center to separate fragile contents. I have seen one gizzard basket made with a handle specifically for use by a horseback rider; it rested snugly at the base of the animal's neck, for carrying eggs safely home.

Two other techniques, less common than the wicker weave, have also been used to produce unusual baskets. The Makah Indians of the Pacific Northwest employ twisting, or twining, to weave their colorful "wabbit" baskets, used to carry home wabbit, or leftovers, from a feast. And the Cherokee Indians make a specialty of plaiting, which is the most complex of the four standard weaving techniques *(page 154)*. I have a particularly handsome double-weave plaited Cherokee basket *(opposite, near right)*. But the finest Indian plaiting I have ever seen was in an Indian shaman's pouch, which a relative of mine found in 1967 in a cottage in upper Michigan. Small enough to be tucked inside the shaman's sash, the pouch was intended for secret medicines and articles of magic. Finding a shaman's pouch is most unusual; customarily it was buried with him. .

In one form of plaiting—the open hexagonal weave—pieces of splint are plaited, over and under, to create a basket with large hexagonal openings. The baskets

The Cherokee double-weave basket, also shown in color on page 153, is actually one basket woven inside another. This is a rare modern example; few basketmakers of today have mastered the technique.

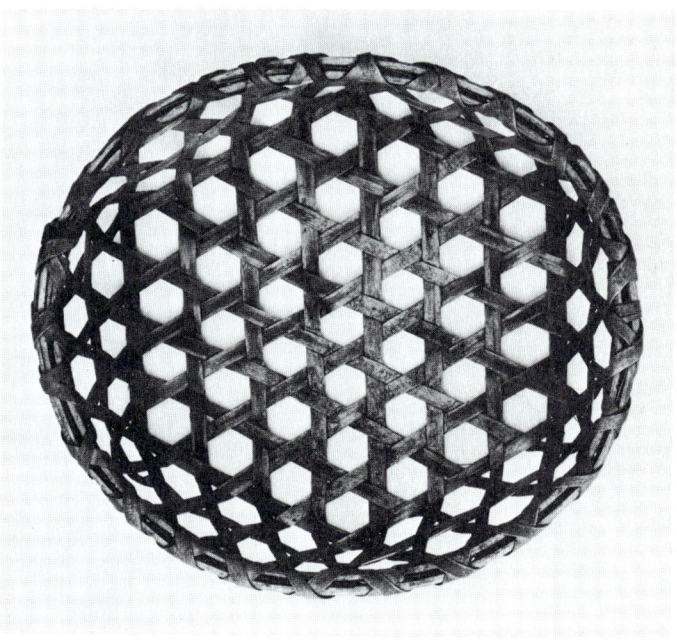

Hexagonal openwork-weave baskets like this one, used in cheese making or to carry shellfish, are rare. A century ago Shakers sold them for 30 cents; today one in good condition could cost $200.

Colored decorations were applied to these two Indian splint baskets by "potato stamping," a process in which colored designs were impressed on the splints with stamps carved from homely materials like potatoes, corncobs or wood. The rectangular basket is known as polychrome because it has three colors. Painted baskets are uncommon and can be expensive. These are from the collection of Kate and Joel Kopp.

Coiled Basketry at Its Best

One special kind of basket, a very desirable collectible, was developed by the Indians of the Southwest as a container for fine-ground meals and flours. Function dictated construction: the container, simply constructed of grass coils, had to be as leakproof as ingenuity could make it.

Coil baskets have no ribs, but rather are built up from the bottom in long spirals stitched together with a flexible wrapping, usually grass. This wrapping is often so closely spaced as to obscure the foundation coil, and sections of it may be dyed to produce patterns of contrasting colors on the basket's surface.

The techniques of coiling are believed to have been developed by the Indians around 7000 B.C. in the Southwest, where game was scarce and the Indians had to rely on grains and fruits for food. Basketry methods used for food storage soon were adapted to crafting utensils such as scoops, and for making sandals and hats as well as trays for gambling games, of which they were fond.

Though coil baskets came to be made elsewhere, they reached a peak of artistry in the Southwest and California. In Arizona, the Apache, Pima and Papagos were preeminent basketmakers; in California, the finest baskets were made by the Washo, Chumash, Tulare, Pomo, Mission, Mono, Kern River Shoshoni and Panamint tribes.

The value of a coil basket depends on many factors: shape, sophistication of design, skill and refinement of execution. Some Indian coil baskets have sold for tens of thousands of dollars, but good ones, newly made, can be found at moderate prices. Most of the older ones are in museums, but the coiling technique has survived in the Southwest, and some choice pieces were made fairly recently. The baskets shown, from Montana Private Collection, date from the late 19th and early 20th centuries.

A patterned tray, with circles like those of a roulette wheel, was made by the Tulare Indians of California for gambling with bones.

BASKETS / 159

The collar-like lip on the container above was much favored by Tulare basketmakers. In this basket, which stands just over 5 inches tall, the broad surface circling the neck is embellished with tiny figures, like a chain of paper dolls.

Large storage vessels called ollas, many of them embellished with designs of people and animals, were made by the Apache of the Southwest. This 3-foot, symmetrically contoured Apache basket is about 100 years old.

Tightly sewn coils mark this exquisite 6½-inch basket, made in 1913 by Dat-So-La-Lee, a woman of the Washo tribe of Nevada.

A coil tray bearing a rattlesnake design is a striking example of the work of southern California's Mission tribe. Many old Indian baskets combine animal and geometric designs. This basket, 21 inches in diameter, is unusual because of its four colors.

160 / BASKETS

look frail but are quite sturdy; at each junction the six splints interlock securely *(page 157)*. Farmers used these baskets, lined with cheesecloth or linen, to drain curds when making cheese, and fishermen carried clams and oysters in them.

The basketry technique known as coiling is often listed as a weave, but it is not. Long coils of fiber—sweet grass, pine needles, rye straw—are wrapped around and around, and stitched together, to shape the basket. The most notable coil baskets are those made as ceremonial pieces by Indians of the West and Southwest, who sometimes spent months on one basket, using as many as 30 stitches to the inch.

You will seldom find old baskets in perfect condition, so before you display them they will need sprucing up. I wash baskets gently with mild soap and warm water, then wipe the basket with a damp sponge to rinse it. If a basket is dry and brittle, I apply a blend of equal parts of boiled linseed oil and turpentine, inside and out. Usually, I do not try to mend damaged baskets; the patch is too conspicuous. But some collectors make repairs, then stain the patch.

Some people like to display baskets by hanging them from the rafters, or by grouping them together on shelves. My own preference is to display them in use. I like to see baskets holding fruit, flowers, plants, hot biscuits or even letters. I try to place them where they fit naturally into the decorative scheme of a room—in small clusters, some on the floor, with the light showing off the texture of the weave and emphasizing their color. Baskets should be pleasant but not overbearing, like people who are good company.

For related material see the articles on Shaker Crafts and Wicker Furniture in separate volumes of this encyclopedia.

A flared wickerwork basket, made of peeled willow, makes an attractive holder for a flowering plant. Older willow baskets acquire a warm patina, in this case polished by sunshine from the window.

MUSEUMS

Farmers' Museum
Cooperstown, New York 13326

The Heard Museum
Phoenix, Arizona 85004

Old Salem Museum
Winston-Salem, North Carolina 27108

Santa Barbara Museum of Natural History
Santa Barbara, California 93105

Shaker Museum
Old Chatham, New York 12136

Smithsonian Institution
Washington, D.C. 20560

BOOKS

Bennett, Ethel, *Splint Basket Making*. University of Arkansas Division of Agriculture and U.S. Department of Agriculture, 1967.

Christopher, F. T., *Basketry*. Dover Publications, Inc., 1952.

Hart, Dan and Carol, *Natural Basketry*. Watson-Guptill Publications, Inc., 1976.

James, George Wharton, *Indian Basketry*. Dover Publications, Inc., 1972.

Ketchum, William C., *American Basketry and Woodenware*. Macmillan Publishing Co., Inc., 1974.

Stephens, Cleo, *Willow Spokes and Wickerwork*. Stackpole Books, 1975.

Teleki, Gloria R., *The Baskets of Rural America*. E. P. Dutton & Co., Inc., 1975.